U. S.
GOVERNMENT
SURPLUS

A Complete Buyer's Manual

FIRST EDITION, JANUARY 1981
SECOND PRINTING, MARCH 1981
THIRD PRINTING, JULY 1981

PUBLISHED BY RAINBOW PUBLISHING COMPANY
P.O. Box 397, CHESTERLAND, OHIO 44026
COPYRIGHT © 1980 BY RAINBOW PUBLISHING CO.

Library of Congress Cataloging in Publication Data
Senay, J.   1937-
    U. S. Government surplus

    Bibliography: p.
    Includes index.
    1. Surplus government property – United States–
Handbooks, manuals, etc. I. Title.
JK1661.S46   353.0071'3045'024658   80-18466
ISBN 0-936218-00-2 Hard Cover
ISBN 0-936218-01-0 Soft Cover

U. S.
GOVERNMENT
SURPLUS

A Complete Buyer's Manual

By J. SENAY

RAINBOW PUBLISHING COMPANY
P.O. BOX 397, CHESTERLAND, OHIO 44026

"LET ALL THINGS BE DONE DECENTLY AND IN ORDER"
I COR. 14:40

I sincerely thank all the people that have made this book possible.
Rex Davis For Professional Editing Contributions
Quality House Printing, Painesville, Ohio For Typesetting
Bill Carnes Publications Services For Jacket Layout

I am deeply indebted to my wife, Donna, for her contributions of editing, writing and material organization.

TABLE OF CONTENTS

Page

CHAPTER 1. **THE LAST GREAT BARGAIN SALE
OF THE CENTURY** **9**
Harold Buck turns sixty cents into $10,000.
Texas farmer bought surplus from the government
for $6.89 and sold it back for $7,200.
An entire city in the U.S. sold as surplus.
Greater opportunity today than ever before.

CHAPTER 2. **HOW TO BUY SURPLUS PROPERTY FROM
THE DEPARTMENT OF DEFENSE**................**11**
Domestic sales.
Consumer type items.
Regional offices listed according to state.
Who may not bid on Department of Defense surplus.
European Region Headquarters and information for:
    Belgium   Holland
    Denmark   Italy
    France   Spain
    Germany   United Kingdom
    Greece
Pacific Region information and listings for:
    Okinawa   Pusan
    Sagami   Subic Bay
    Thailand   Australia
    Bupyong   Hawaii
    Guam   Clark
    Iwakuni   Misawa

CHAPTER 3. **HOW TO IMPORT DEPARTMENT OF DEFENSE
SURPLUS PROPERTY** **17**
Information on "Foreign Excess Property Import
Determination" (Form DIB 302P).
Department of Commerce Bureau for obtaining
complete information on importing regulations
and sample forms.

CHAPTER 4.   HOW TO BUY SURPLUS PROPERTY FROM THE
             GENERAL SERVICES ADMINISTRATION (G.S.A.) 19
             Regional offices listed by state.
             Who may not bid on G.S.A. surplus.

CHAPTER 5.   HOW TO BUY CONTRACTOR INVENTORY 21
             Eleven Defense Contract Administration Offices
                selling construction material, machinery and
                equipment.
             Sixteen Department of the Navy Activities
                selling contractor inventory.

CHAPTER 6.   SALES METHODS USED BY
             GOVERNMENT AGENCIES. .27
             Procedure for submitting a Sealed Bid.
             Procedure for submitting a Spot Bid.
             Bid Deposits and Payments.
             How to obtain an "Annual Bid Deposit Bond".
             Procedure for Auctions.
             Procedure for Negotiated Sales.
             Retail Sales.

CHAPTER 7.   BIDDERS SERVICE COMPANIES. 31
             Listing of companies that assist bidders
                with the following:
                   Inspections   Telephone Information
                   Photographs   Shipping Arrangements
                   Bid Placement

CHAPTER 8.   HOW TO OBTAIN TECHNICAL MANUALS 33
             Instructions for obtaining technical manuals
                for equipment issued to the following:
                   Army   Air Force
                   Navy   G.S.A.
             Where to obtain Field Manual for World War II
                period equipment.
             Where to obtain publications for equipment of
                the most recent period.
             How to obtain obsolete publications of
                government technical manuals.

6

CHAPTER 9.   HELPFUL GOVERNMENT PUBLICATIONS. 35
                    Where to obtain:
                        Military Specifications
                        Military Standards
                        Federal Specifications
                        Federal Standards
                        Qualified Product Lists
                        Industry Documents
                        Military Handbooks
                        Guide For Private Industry

CHAPTER 10.   HOW TO IDENTIFY ELECTRONIC EQUIPMENT 37
                    The Joint Electronics Type Designation System (JETDS)
                    Designations for Systems, Centers and Sets
                    Designations for Groups
                    Designations for Units

CHAPTER 11.   GOVERNMENT SURPLUS DONATION PROGRAM 47
                    Types of surplus donated.
                    How donable Federal Surplus is distributed.
                    Who is eligible to receive donated government surplus.
                    Government agencies eligible.
                    Non-profit educational and public health activities eligible.
                    Educational activities of special interest
                        to the Armed Forces eligible.
                    Public airports eligible.
                    Ten regional offices coordinating
                        Surplus Donation Program.
                    Fifty-four storage points for Surplus Donation
                        Program listed by state.

CHAPTER 12.   UNITED STATES CUSTOMS SERVICE AUCTIONS. 57
                    Information for forty cities.

CHAPTER 13.   UNITED STATES POSTAL SERVICE AUCTIONS. 59
                    Information for nineteen Dead Parcel Branches.

CHAPTER 14.   BUYING SURPLUS PROPERTY FROM
              THE CANADIAN GOVERNMENT. 61
                  Six Regional Offices:
                      Pacific Region   National Capital Region
                      Prairie Region   Quebec Region
                      Ontario Region   Atlantic Region
                  Sale methods including:
                      Sealed Bid
                      Public Auction
                      Retail Cash and Carry Sale
                  Who may not bid on Canadian Government
                      surplus material.

CHAPTER 15.   PACKING AND SHIPPING. .63
                  A listing of over two hundred and thirty companies
                  furnishing crating, freight, packing, water trans-
                  portation and inspection; organized by state and
                  one hundred and seventy Defense Disposal Sites
                  that they now service.

CHAPTER 16.   ITEMS SOLD AS SURPLUS BY
              THE DEPARTMENT OF DEFENSE. 93
                  Thousands of items that are sold by the government
                  as surplus, alphabetically listed by major
                  heading and class.

INDEX 117

BIBLIOGRAPHY

CHAPTER 1

THE LAST GREAT BARGAIN SALE OF THE CENTURY

Whatever your business, whatever your hobby, if you are looking for items new or used, chances are the government has what you want for sale, right now and at prices you thought you had seen for the last time twenty years ago. This book is written for those who want to take full advantage of this opportunity. It is a manual of information for the person or organization that wants to save and make money on what is probably the last great bargain sale of the century.

Today the opportunities in government surplus are greater by far than they ever were in the past. That's right, greater by far! The government sells over $1 billion (original cost to the government) worth of surplus yearly. After World War II, the government was very restrictive and would not allow the general public to bid on surplus. Today, however, all that has changed. The "secret" is out and the general public (even non-citizens) has the opportunity to bid for government surplus on an equal basis with any company or individual, and the majority of items being offered for sale are in quantities with which an average person may easily deal. For example, there have been items listed for sale that have received winning bids of only pennies. In sale book after sale book, which you can obtain free, the government sells thousands of items listed as unused and in good condition. Some time ago, Harold Buck placed a bid on "60 Peloruses" listed in a government surplus sales catalog. He did not know what they were so he decided to take a chance and enter a bid of one cent each. His bid, as it turned out, was highest. Not long after Harold took possession, officials in Washington found that the navigational instruments Harold had bought for 60 cents were worth $10,000. In another case, a Texas farmer bought a lot of 168 aircraft computers for $6.89. He thought they were some kind of cardboard slide rules. The computers, however, were electronic fire-control instruments worth $7,200 each. He ended up selling them back to the government for $63,000. For another instance, the

9

Federal Government built the town of Passamaquoddy, Maine as the site for a proposed power project. The project was terminated and the town was put on the auction block and gobbled up at a fraction of its original cost.

CHAPTER 2

HOW TO BUY SURPLUS PROPERTY FROM
THE DEPARTMENT OF DEFENSE

Domestic Sales

There are sales offices, both foreign and domestic, which sell Defense Department surplus property. This surplus includes all the items listed in Chapter 16. Prospective buyers who wish to bid on items offered for sale through the four sales offices located within the United States (excluding Hawaii) may do so by writing to each sales region in which they are interested. The sales regions are listed later in this chapter. Time and energy may be saved, however, by writing to the central office which co-ordinates all four United States sales regions.

DOD Surplus Sales
P.O. Box 1370
Battle Creek, Mich. 49016

Request an application for placement on the bidders list. This application provides a place to indicate the types of property and the regional sales offices in which the prospective bidder is interested. The prospective bidders name will then be recorded on the bidders list and a bidders identification card and bidders number will be issued. When the types of property selected on the application are placed for sale in the location indicated, a sale catalog called an "Invitation for Bids" (IFB) will be mailed.

Domestic Sales Consumer Type Items

Prospective bidders who have an interest only in consumer type items such as furniture, typewriters, office machines, automobiles and the like, enhance their chances of obtaining such property by participating in local sales. These sales are limited to the areas where the property is located and require bidders to be present to participate. For information pertaining to these sales, contact the regional offices below.

11

Regional Office

Defense Property Disposal Region
P.O. Box 14716
Memphis, Tenn. 38114

Serving

Alabama, Tennessee, Georgia, Texas, Louisiana, North Carolina, Kentucky, South Carolina, Arkansas, Mississippi, New Mexico, Oklahoma, Puerto Rico, Florida

Regional Office

Defense Property Disposal Region
P.O. Box 13110
Columbus, Ohio 43213

Serving

New York, Wisconsin, Michigan, Pennsylvania, Nebraska, Kansas, Indiana, Illinois, Iowa, Missouri, Minnesota, Maryland, Ohio, Virginia, New Jersey, Massachusetts, Washington, D. C., Maine, Delaware, Rhode Island, New Hampshire, Vermont, Connecticut, West Virginia.

Regional Office

Defense Property Disposal Region
P.O. Box 58
Defense Depot Ogden Station
Ogden, Utah 84401

Serving

South Dakota, Colorado, Utah, Washington, Idaho, Montana, California, Arizona, Oregon, Alaska, North Dakota, Nevada, Wyoming

Who May Not Bid on Department of Defense Surplus

1. Those under 18 years of age.
2. A member of the armed forces of the United States, including the United States Coast Guard or a civilian employee of the Department of Defense or the United States Coast Guard and whose duties include any function of supervisory responsibility for or within the defense property disposal program.
3. An agent, employee or immediate member of the household of personnel in (2) above.

European Region, Department of Defense

To bid on items offered for sale in Portugal, Belgium, Greece, Denmark, Great Britain, France, Germany, Netherlands, Italy and Spain, write to:

> Defense Property Disposal Region-Europe
> Attn: DPDR—EMM
> APO New York
> New York 09633

Ask for the bidders list application.

For assistance in locating packers, shippers and other information, write to the following:

Belgium:

U.S. Commercial Attache, Mr. Edward E. Keller,
> Boulevard du Regent, 27,
> B 1000 Brussels, Belgium

Denmark:

American Embassy, U.S. Commercial Attache,
> Mr. E. J. Rankin,
> Dag Hammerskjold Alle 24,
> DK 2100 Copenhagen, Denmark

France:

American Embassy, Commercial Attache,
2 Avenue Gabriel,
F75008 Paris, France

Germany:

American Embassy, Mehlemer Aue.,
D5300 Bad Godesberg, Germany

Greece:

American Embassy, Commercial Attache,
91, Vassilisis Sophias Avenue,
Athens, Greece

Holland:

Atlantic NB Amsterdam-O, Cruguiusweg 25,
Gemeentelijk Handels,
Entrepot, Holland

Italy:

Mincomes, (Ministry of Foreign Commerce),
Roma, Italy

Spain:

American Embassy, Commercial Attache,
Serrano 75,
Madrid, Spain

United Kingdom:

The Economic Defense Attache,
American Embassy, P.O. Box 444,
Grosvenor Grove, London W. 1, England

Pacific Region, Department of Defense

To bid on items offered for sale in Japan, Okinawa, Guam, Korea, Philippines, Thailand or Hawaii write to:

DOD Surplus Sales
P.O. Box 1370
Battle Creek, Mich. 49016

Ask for the "Surplus/Foreign Excess Personal Property Bidders Application."

For assistance in locating packers and shippers and other information, write to the following:

Chief, DPDO Okinawa, Box 5107, APO San Fransisco 96248

Chief, DPDO Sagami, APO San Francisco 96343

Chief, DPDO Thailand, APO San Francisco 96346

Chief, DPDO Bupyong, APO San Francisco 96483

Chief, DPDO Guam, Box 190, FPO San Francisco 96630

Chief, DPDO Iwakuni, FPO Seattle 98764

Chief, DPDO Pusan, APO San Francisco 96259

Chief, DPDO Subic Bay, Box 40, FPO San Francisco 96651

Chief, DPDO Australia, FPO San Francisco 96680

Chief, DPDO Clark, APO San Francisco 96274

Chief, DPDO Hawaii, Box 300, Pearl Harbor, Hawaii 96860

Chief, DPDO Misawa, APO San Francisco 96519

DEPARTMENT OF DEFENSE
DEFENSE LOGISTICS AGENCY

SALE NO. 01- 9001

BID OPENING:

1 AUG   **10:00 A.M.**

SEALED BID

Offering...

MILITARY

escape & evasion kits

which contain

★ **COINS**
★ **RINGS**
★ **CHAINS**

SALE SITE:

DEFENSE PROPERTY DISPOSAL SERVICE
50 NORTH WASHINGTON STREET
FEDERAL CENTER • AUDITORIUM NO. 1
BATTLE CREEK, MICHIGAN 49016

FOR FURTHER INFORMATION SEE INSIDE

CHAPTER 3

HOW TO IMPORT DEPARTMENT OF DEFENSE SURPLUS PROPERTY LOCATED OUTSIDE THE CONTINENTAL UNITED STATES

To bid on department of defense surplus property located outside of the above areas for import into the United States, Hawaii, Alaska, Puerto Rico and the Virgin Islands, follow the procedure described below.

Fill out a "Foreign Excess Property Import Determination" (Form DIB 302P). This is a very simple form which will allow the Department of Commerce to determine if the property is truly government surplus and allowed to be imported. The applicant need not own the property to file for an import determination, however, the application must relate to a specific lot of property which has been or is to be acquired in a single transaction.

If the property is being offered for sale by a U.S. Government agency, submission of the (Form DIB 302P) should result in receiving the import determination before the deadline for bid submission. While it is not always possible, such applications are given priority in processing.

When ownership of the property is acquired the applicant fills out (Form DIB 304P) in duplicate and submits it to the federal excess property office with proof of ownership and a copy of the F.E.P. import determination.

Foreign excess property will be cleared for entry into the United States only upon presentation to the U.S. customs of an F.E.P. import determination.

For complete information on importing foreign excess property including regulations and sample forms, write to:

Foreign Excess Property Officer
Office of Import Programs
U.S. Department of Commerce
Washington, D.C. 20230

DEPARTMENT OF DEFENSE
DEFENSE SUPPLY AGENCY
SALE NO. 27-9247

BID OPENING:

17 July   — 9:00 A.M.

SEALED
BID station wagons

trucks

Offering...

VEHICLES

semitrailers

buses

sedans

COLUMBUS, OHIO
DPDR

FOR SALE SITE AND MAILING ADDRESS
SEE PAGE NO. 35

FOR FURTHER INFORMATION SEE INSIDE

CHAPTER 4

HOW TO BUY SURPLUS PROPERTY FROM
THE GENERAL SERVICES ADMINISTRATION (GSA)

There are twelve regional sales offices which sell general services administration surplus property. You may bid on the surplus offered for sale in any one region or all of the regions.

The items offered for sale are similar to those mentioned in Chapter 16. You may be put on the bidders list in as many of the regions as you wish, but you must write to each regional office individually stating that you wish to be placed on the bidders list. Here is a list of the regional offices:

Write to: General Services Administration
Federal Supply Service
Personal Property Division

John W. McCormac
Post Office and Courthouse
Boston, MA 02109 (Area includes: Connecticut, Maine, Massachusetts, New Hampshire, Rhode Island, Vermont)

26 Federal Plaza
New York, NY 10007 (Area includes: New Jersey, New York, Puerto Rico, Virgin Islands)

7th & D Streets, SW
Washington, DC 20407 (Area includes: Delaware, District of Columbia, Maryland, Pennsylvania, Virginia, West Virginia)

1776 Peachtree Street, NW
Atlanta, GA 30309 (Area includes: Alabama, Florida, Georgia, Kentucky, Mississippi, North Carolina, South Carolina, Tennessee)

230 South Dearborn Street
Chicago, IL 60604 (Area includes: Illinois, Indiana, Michigan, Minnesota, Ohio, Wisconsin)

Alaskan area
P.O. Box 1632
Anchorage, Alaska 99510

1500 E. Bannister Road
Kansas City, MO 64131 (Area includes: Iowa, Kansas, Missouri, Nebraska)

819 Taylor Street
Fort Worth, TX 76102 (Area includes: Arkansas, Louisiana, New Mexico, Oklahoma, Texas)

Denver Federal Center, Bldg. 41
Denver, CO 80225 (Area includes: Colorado, Montana, North Dakota, South Dakota, Utah, Wyoming)

525 Market Street
San Francisco, CA 94105 (Area includes: Arizona, California, Nevada)

Hawaiian area
Federal Building
300 Ala Moana Blvd.
Honolulu, HI 96813

GSA Center
Auburn WA 98002 (Area includes: Idaho, Oregon, Washington)

Who May Not Bid on (GSA) General Services Administration Surplus

1. Those under 18 years of age.
2. An employee of an agency of the Federal Government (either as a civilian or as a member of the armed forces of the United States, including the United States Coast Guard, on active duty) prohibited by the regulations of that agency from purchasing property sold hereunder.
3. An agent or immediate member of the household of the employee in (2) above.

CHAPTER 5

HOW TO BUY CONTRACTOR INVENTORY

There are special regions set up to sell contractor inventory, including Department of the Navy activities which have been declared surplus. Private individuals may bid on the inventory in any one or in all of the regions. The items offered for sale are similar to those mentioned in Chapter 16. Of course, most of the property will be the type used in construction. Prospective bidders must write to each regional office individually requesting to be placed on the bidders list and to receive "Invitations for Bids" (IFB). Here is a list of the regional offices:

Commander
Defense Contract Administration Services Region, Atlanta
3100 Maple Drive, NE
Atlanta, Georgia 30305

Commander
Defense Contract Administration Services Region, Boston
666 Summer Street
Boston, Massachusetts 02210

Commander
Defense Contract Administration Services Region, Chicago
O'Hare International Airport
P.O. Box 66475
Chicago, Illinois 60666

Commander
Defense Contract Administration Services Region, Cleveland
1240 E. Ninth Street
Cleveland, Ohio 44199

Commander
Defense Contract Administration Services Region, Dallas
500 South Ervay Street
Dallas, Texas 75201

Commander
Defense Contract Administration Services Region, Detroit
1580 East Grand Blvd.
Detroit, Michigan 48211

Commander
Defense Contract Administration Services Region, Philadelphia
P.O. Box 7478
Philadelphia, Pennsylvania 19101

Commander
Defense Contract Administration Services Region, St. Louis
1136 Washington Avenue
St. Louis, Missouri 63101

Commander
Defense Contract Administration Services Region, Los Angeles
11099 South LaCienega Blvd.
Los Angeles, California 90045

Commander
Defense Contract Administration Services Region, New York
60 Hudson Street
New York, New York 10013

Commander
Defense Contract Administration Services Region, San Francisco
866 Malcolm Road
Burlingame, California 94010

Department of the Navy Activities Monitoring Sales of Contractor Inventory

Naval Plant Representative
Naval Plant Representative Office
Goodyear Aerospace Corporation
Akron, Ohio 44305

Naval Plant Representative
Naval Plant Representative Office
Grumman Aerospace Corporation
Bethpage, L.I., New York 11714

Naval Plant Representative
Naval Plant Representative Office
Lockheed Aircraft Corporation
Burbank, California 91503

Naval Plant Representative
Naval Plant Representative Office
North American Rockwell Corporation
4300 East Fifth Avenue
Columbus, Ohio 43216

Naval Plant Representative
Naval Plant Representative Office
LTV Aerospace Corporation
Vought Aeronautics Division
P.O. Box 5907
Dallas Texas 75222

Naval Plant Representative
Naval Plant Representative Office
Sperry Gyroscope Company
Great Neck, L. I., New York 11020

Naval Plant Representative
Naval Plant Representative Office
Applied Physics Laboratory
Johns Hopkins Road
Laurel, Maryland 20810

Naval Plant Representative
Naval Plant Representative Office
McDonnell Douglas Corporation
Long Beach, California 90801

Naval Plant Representative
Naval Plant Representative Office
(Special Projects Office)
General Electric Company
Ordnance Department
100 Plastics Avenue
Pittsfield, Massachusetts 01201

Naval Plant Branch Representative Office
Hercules, Inc., Bachus Works
P.O. Box 157
Magna, Utah 84044

Naval Plant Representative
Naval Plant Representative Office
Applied Physics Laboratory
Johns Hopkins University
8621 Georgia Avenue
Silver Spring, Maryland 20910

Naval Plant Representative
Naval Plant Representative Office
General Dynamics Pomona Division
1675 W. Mission Boulevard
P.O. Box 2507
Pomona, California 91766

Naval Plant Representative
Naval Plant Representative Office
(Special Projects Office)
Lockheed Missiles and Space Company
P.O. Box 504
Sunnyvale, California 94088

Naval Plant Representative
Naval Plant Representative Office
Sikorsky Aircraft Division
Stratford, Connecticut 06497

Supervisor of Shipbuilding, Conversion and Repair, USN
Pascagoula, MS 39567

Supervisor of Shipbuilding, Conversion and Repair, USN
Groton, Connecticut 06340

Supervisor of Shipbuilding, Conversion and Repair, USN
Newport News Shipbuilding & Drydock Co.
Newport News, VA 23607

DEPARTMENT OF DEFENSE
DEFENSE LOGISTICS AGENCY

SALE NO. 27-9313

BID OPENING:

18 SEP   -9:00 A.M.

Offering...

OFFICE MACHINES

&

EQUIPMENT

OFFICE & HOUSEHOLD

FURNITURE

S E A L E D BID

FOR SALE SITE AND MAILING
ADDRESS SEE PAGE NO. 39

FOR FURTHER INFORMATION SEE INSIDE

Sample cover of U.S. Government Sale Catalog

CHAPTER 6

SALES METHODS USED BY GOVERNMENT AGENCIES

There are five sales methods used by government agencies to sell surplus property: sealed bid (the most common), spot bid, auction, negotiated sale and retail sale. This chapter describes these methods and offers some additional information to assist the prospective bidder.

Sealed Bid

In a sealed bid sale, the prospective bidder receives, by mail, a sales catalog "Invitation for Bids" that lists and describes the surplus property for sale. This catalog also identifies the place where the sale will be held, gives the location of the surplus property, tells when the property may be inspected, gives the date and time of the sale and the name of the person in charge. The catalogs are mailed well in advance of the sale date, so there should be ample time to inspect the property if desired. In addition, each catalog contains a bid form and complete instructions. The bidder fills in the item number and the bid amount and then returns the form.

All bids must be accompanied by a "Bid Deposit." This is usually 20% of the bid amount. As an example, if the bid is $100 for a car, the bidder sends a check for $20 with the bid. If the bid is not successful, the check will be returned uncashed. If the bid is successful, the "Bid Deposit" will be counted as part of the purchase price. Those who plan to bid frequently should consider using an "Annual Bid Deposit Bond." It has some very obvious advantages! (1) No bid deposit will be required; (2) money is not tied up, pending return of unsuccessful bid deposits; (3) it eliminates writing checks or obtaining money orders and the record keeping they require. For more information about "Annual Bid Deposit Bonds" write to:

Defense Property Disposal Service
Attn: DPDS—MCC—P
Federal Center
Battle Creek, Mich. 49016

27

All bidders will receive by mail, a list of the successful bidders along with their addresses, a list of the items on which they have bid and the dollar amount of their successful bid.

Unsuccessful bidders are not out any money (except their postage cost). The bid deposit will be returned and the catalog "Invitation for Bids," is free, as is the privilege of submitting a bid and the list of successful bidders. Successful bidders on a sealed bid are required to pay the balance and remove the property within the time period specified by the government. This is usually one month after written notice is mailed.

Spot Bid

In a spot bid sale, the prospective bidder receives by mail, a sales catalog that lists and describes the surplus property for sale. This catalog also identifies the place where the sale will be held, gives the location of the surplus property, tells when the property may be inspected, gives the date and the time of the sale and the name, as well as, address and phone number of person in charge. The catalogs are mailed well in advance of the sale date so there should be ample time to inspect the property if desired.

Participants may be present or may submit a bid by mail. Bids sent in by mail to the spot bid sale will be required to include a deposit which is usually 20% of the bid; just the same as the rules for a sealed bid sale. Successful bidders present at the spot bid sale will be required to make a partial payment of at least 20% of the sale price; just the same as the rules for an auction sale. Payment of the balance and removal of the property is usually required within one month after the sale.

Auction

In an auction sale, as in the case of the spot bid sale above, the prospective bidder receives, by mail, a sales catalog that lists and describes the surplus property for sale. This catalog also identifies the place where the sale will be held, gives the location of the surplus property, tells when the property may be inspected, gives the date and time of the sale and the name, as well as, the address and phone number of the person in charge. The catalogs are mailed well in advance of the sale date so there should be ample time to inspect the property if desired. In an auction type sale, the bidder must be present to participate. No mailed-in bids will be accepted.

Of course, the successful bidder at an auction will know immediately and will be required to make a partial payment of at least 20% of the sale price. The balance of the sale price and the removal of the property is usually required within one month after the auction.

Negotiated Sale

States, municipalities, territories, possessions, political subdivisions or tax supported agencies therein may submit a list of specific items they want to the nearest defense property disposal region. This is known as a negotiated sale. They will then be notified if the items they want are available and what the sale price would be.

The public may purchase by negotiated sale in certain limited circumstances. For further information, write to your nearest defense property disposal region.

Retail Sales

At retail sales, small quantities of individual items are offered for sale at fixed prices, just as in a flea market. Those interested in this type of sale, should contact their nearest defense property disposal region office and ask which military installations conduct retail sales.

DEPARTMENT OF DEFENSE

DEFENSE LOGISTICS AGENCY

SALE NO. 31-9295

BID OPENING:

7 AUG   9:00 A.M.

SEALED
BID

Offering...

CALCULATORS
TYPEWRITERS
CASH REGISTERS
INSTRUMENTS &
LABORATORY EQUIPMENT

Sample cover of U.S. Government Sale Catalog

FOR SALE SITE & MAILING ADDRESS SEE PAGE 33

FOR FURTHER INFORMATION SEE INSIDE

CHAPTER 7

BIDDERS SERVICE COMPANIES

The government guarantees, within limits, that the items listed in their sales catalogs will be "as described." If, however, additional information is required, there are private companies which will inspect and verify the condition of the item, look for parts which may need special consideration, take photographs, place a bid, telephone information as to who the high bidder was on a particular sale, make shipping arrangements and, in short, help in just about any way needed.

Remember, these companies are privately owned and are not a part of the government. They will want a fee for their services. I suggest that you write them a letter and ask which services they perform and what their fee is.

Some of these companies are listed below:

Donna's Bid Reporting Service, 1193 N. 2000 W, Clinton, UT 84403
Pak-N-Ship, P.O. Box 217, Clearfield, UT 84015
Kelly Services, 100 East Broad St., Columbus, OH 43215
Computor Data Systems, Inc., 6950 Worthington-Galena Rd.,
     Worthington, OH 43085
Manpower, Inc., 4938 Poplar Ave., Memphis, TENN 38117
Mr. Bob Stevens, 4453 Airways, Memphis, TENN 38116

In addition to the above, you could contact the office of any temporary help company located near the sale item.

Sample cover of U.S. Government Sale Catalog

DEPARTMENT OF DEFENSE
DEFENSE LOGISTICS AGENCY

SALE NO. 31-8428

BID OPENING:

26 SEPT   9:00 A.M.

SEALED BID

Offering...

- BED
- DESK
- CLOTHING
- MATTRESS
- COMPRESSOR
- AMMUNITION BOX
- REFRIGERATION EQUIPMENT

For sale site and mailing
          address see page   no. 43

FOR FURTHER INFORMATION SEE INSIDE

CHAPTER 8

HOW TO OBTAIN TECHNICAL MANUALS

The government has printed technical manuals and maintenance manuals for almost all equipment issued to the armed forces. This instruction material is well written and provides complete information for each piece of equipment. To obtain a technical manual, you may have to try a few different sources. The best procedure would be to record all the information that you can about the equipment, such as equipment designation, component number, manufacturers name, etc. Then with this information, write to the appropriate branch of the armed services and ask for a technical manual or at least ask for the correct technical manual number.

ARMY

Commander
U.S. Army Adjutant General Publications Center
1655 Woodson Rd.
St. Louis, MO 63114

NAVY

Commander
Naval Publications and Forms Center
Attn: Cash Sales
5801 Tabor Ave.
Philadelphia, PA 19120

AIR FORCE

Headquarters
United States Air Force
USAF/LEY
Washington, D.C. 20330

The printing branch of the national archives now has custody of the military publications formerly accumulated by the government printing office. This includes an unusually extensive collection of technical manuals, which recent increments have made the largest now in existence. For information on these write to:

G.S.A.
National Archives
and Records Service
Washington, D.C. 20408

The volume of material requires that they have specific requests by manual number and date before they will tell you the cost of the publications. Thousands of listings of technical manuals can be found in Field Manual 21-6 (for the World War II period) and Department of the Army pamphlet 310-4 (the most recent). These publications are at most large public libraries.

Pamphlet 310-4 "Index of Technical Publications" may also be purchased from Department of the Army, U.S. Army AG Publ. Center, 2800 Eastern Blvd., Baltimore, Maryland, 21220.

Requests for obsolete publications with issue dates prior to 1954 should be forwarded to the Director, National Archives and Records Service (NNG), GSA, Washington, D.C. 20409.

Requests for obsolete publications with issue dates later than 1954 should be forwarded to Department of the Army, Attn: DAAG—AMR, Washington, D.C. 20314.

CHAPTER 9

HELPFUL GOVERNMENT PUBLICATIONS

The Naval Publications and Forms Center (NPFC). Philadelphia, is the Department of Defense Single Stock Point (DOD—SSP) and distribution center for unclassified specifications and standards utilized throughout the Department of Defense for military procurement.

The documents stocked and distributed by this agency are:
(1) Military Specifications, (2) Military Standards, (3) Federal Specifications, (4) Federal Standards, (5) Qualified Products Lists, (6) Industry Documents, (7) Military Handbooks, (8) Air Force-Navy Aeronautical Standards, (9) Air Force-Navy Aeronautical Design Standards, (10) Air Force-Navy Aeronautical Specifications, (11) U.S. Air Force Specifications.

"A Guide for Private Industry" is a pamphlet put out by this agency which explains their services in more depth.

Naval Publications and Forms Center
5801 Tabor Ave.
Philadelphia, PA 19120

The following listings of government publications may be obtained from the superintendent of documents without charge.

Publication (SB—231) Government Specifications, Federal Standards, Drawings and Indexes
Publication (SB—129) Procurement, Supply Cataloging and Classification
Publication (SB—141) Federal Government

DEPARTMENT OF DEFENSE
DEFENSE LOGISTICS AGENCY

SALE NO. 41-9006

BID OPENING:

31 OCTOBER   **9:00 AM**

SEALED BID

Offering... **HAND TOOLS**   **CONTAINERS**

HOSE & FITTINGS   **HARDWARE**   **OFFICE MACHINES**

REFRIGERATION & AIR CONDITIONING EQUIPMENT

METALWORKING MACHINERY   **CLOTHING & TEXTILES**

PUMPS AND COMPRESSORS   **PLUMBING & HEATING**

FIRE FIGHTING EQUIPMENT

PHOTOGRAPHIC EQUIPMENT

SALE SITE:

FOR SALE SITE AND MAILING ADDRESS SEE PAGE 39

FOR FURTHER INFORMATION SEE INSIDE

CHAPTER 10

HOW TO IDENTIFY ELECTRONIC EQUIPMENT

The Joint Electronics Type Designation System (JETDS) formerly known as the "AN" nomenclature system, is used to designate electronic equipment.

1. Designations for Systems, Centers and Sets

These are identified by using Table 1 "Equipment Indicators." The letters that follow "AN/" indicate (1) equipment installation; (2) type of equipment; (3) purpose of equipment. For example: AN/VRC-12, represents a radio communication set installed in a vehicle designated for functions other than carrying electronic equipment, such as tanks and jeeps.

2. Designations for Groups

These are identified by using Table 2 "Group Indicators." All groups, including commercial "off the shelf" equipment, will be identified by a two letter indicator. For example: "OD" indicates indicator group. Where applicable, additional equipment indicator letters following a slash (/) may be selected from Table 1. For example: OD-311/GPS-4 indicates indicator group, general ground use installation, radar, used for detecting and/or range and bearing search.

3. Designations for Units

These are identified by using Table 3 "Unit Indicators." The type designation for units having one end use consists of a unit indicator from Table 3, a dash, a number, a slash and the equipment indicators it is used with from Table 1. As an example: The receiver used with the AN/VRC-12 would be indicated as R-40/VCR-12.

If you are going to be an active bidder on electronic equipment, it would be wise to send for the complete publication of the "Joint

Electronics Type Designation System." This may be obtained from:

Commanding Officer
U.S. Naval Publications and Forms Center
5801 Tabor Ave.
Philadelphia, PA 19120

Ask for Document "MIL-STD-196C."

TABLE 1 — EQUIPMENT INDICATORS

Installation (1st letter)

A-Piloted aircraft	S-Water
B Underwater mobile, submarine	T-Ground, transportable
D-Pilotless carrier	U-General utility
F-Fixed ground	V-Ground, vehicular
G-General ground use	W Water surface and under
K-Amphibious	water combination
M-Ground, mobile	Z-Piloted and pilotless
P-Portable	airborne vehicle combination

Type of Equipment (2nd letter)

A-Invisible light, heat radiation	P-Radar
C-Carrier	Q-Sonar and underwater sound
D-Radiac	R-Radio
G-Telegraph or teletype	S-Special types, magnetic, etc.,
I-Interphone and public address	or combinations of types
J-Electromechanical or	T-Telephone (wire)
Inertial wire covered	V-Visual and visible light
K-Telemetering	W-Armament (peculiar to arma-
L-Countermeasures	ment, not otherwise covered)
M-Meteorological	X-Facsimile or television
N-Sound in air	Y-Data processing

Purpose (3rd letter)

B-Bombing
C-Communications (receiving and transmitting
D-Direction finder reconnaissance and/or surveillance
E-Ejection and/or release
G-Fire Control, or searchlight directing
H-Recording and/or reproducing (graphic meteorological and sound)
K-Computing
M-Maintenance and/or test assemblies (including tools)

N-Navigational aids (including altimeters, beacons, compasses, racons, depth, sounding approach and landing)
Q-Special, or combination of purposes
R-Receiving, passive detecting
S-Detecting and/or range and bearing, search
T-Transmitting
W-Automatic flight or remote control
X-Identification and recognition

Miscellaneous Identification

X,Y,Z-Changes in voltage, phase, or frequency
T-Training
(V)-Variable grouping

TABLE 2 – GROUP INDICATORS

Comp Ind.	Family Name	Example of Use (not to be construed as limiting the application of the unit indicator)
OA	Miscellaneous groups	Groups not otherwise classified. Do not use if a more specific indicator, such as OD, OE, OG, etc., applies.
OB	Multiplexer and/or demultiplexer groups	Multiplexer groups, demultiplexer groups, composites thereof.

39

OD	Indicator groups	All types.
OE	Antenna groups	All types.
OF	Adapter groups	All types.
OG	Amplifier groups	All types.
OH	Simulator groups	All types.
OJ	Consoles and console groups	All types.
OK	Control groups	All types.
OL	Data analysis and data processing groups	All types.
OM	Modulator and/or demodulator groups	Modulator groups, demodulator groups, composites thereof.
ON	Interconnecting groups	All types.
OP	Power Supply groups	All types.
OQ	Test Set groups	All types.
OR	Receiver groups	All types.
OT	Transmitter groups	All types.
OU	Converter groups	All types.
OV	Generator groups	All types excluding power generating equipment.
OW	Terminal groups	Telegraph, telephone, radio etc.
OX	Coder, decoder, interrogator, transponder groups	All types.
OY	Radar Set groups	Do not use if a more specific indicator, such as OE, OR, OT, etc., applies
OZ	Radio Set groups	Do not use if a more specific indicator, such as OE, OR, OT, etc., applies.

Table 3 on following pages.

TABLE 3 — UNIT INDICATORS

Comp Ind.	Family Name	Example of Use (not to be construed as limiting the application of the unit indicator)
AB	Supports, antenna	Antenna mounts, mast bases, mast sections, towers, etc.
AM	Amplifiers	Power, audio, interphone, radio frequency, video, electronic control, etc.
AS	Antennae, simple and complex	Arrays, parabolic type, masthead, whip or telescopic loop, dipole, reflector, etc.
BA	Battery, primary type	B batteries, battery packs, etc.
BB	Battery, secondary type	Storage batteries, battery packs, etc.
BZ	Alarm units	All types.
C	Controls	Control box, remote tuning controls, etc.
CG	Cable assemblies, RF	RF Cables, wave guides, transmission lines, etc., with terminals.
CM	Comparators	Compares two or more input signals.
CN	Compensators	Electrical and/or mechanical compensating, regulating or attenuating apparatus.
CP	Computers	A mechanical and/or electronic mathematical calculating device.
CU	Couplers	Impedance coupling devices, directional couplers, etc.
CV	Converters (electronic)	Electronic apparatus for changing the phase, frequency, or from "one" medium to "another".
CW	Radomes	Radomes

CX Cable assemblies, non RF   Non RF cables with terminals, test leads, also composite cables of RF and non RF conductors.

CY Cases and cabinets   Rigid and semirigid structure for enclosing or carrying equipment.

D   Dispensers   Chaff

DA Load, dummy   RF and non RF test loads.

DT Detecting heads   Magnetic pickup device, search coil, hydrophone, etc.

F   Filter units   Electronic types; band pass, low pass, band suppression, noise telephone, filter networks; excludes non-reparable types.

FR Frequency measuring device   Frequency meters, tuned cavity, etc.

G   Generators, power   Electrical power generators without prime movers (See PU).

H   Head, hand, and chest sets   Includes earphone.

HD Environmental apparatus   Heating, cooling, dehumidifying, pressure, vacum devices, etc.

ID Indicator units, non-cathode-ray tube   Calibrated dials and meters, indicating lights, etc. (See IP).

IM Intensity measuring devices   Includes SWR gear, field intensity and noise meters, slotted lines, etc.

IP Indicator units, cathode-ray tube   Azimuth, elevation, panoramic, etc.

J   Interface units   Interconnecting and junction units, etc. Do not use if a more specific indicator applies.

KY Keying devices   Mechanical, electrical and electronic keyer coders, interrupters, etc.

LS Loudspeakers   Separately housed loudspeakers, intercommunication stations.

M	Microphones	Radio, telephone, throat, hand, etc.
MD	Modulators, demodulators, discriminators	Device for varying amplitude, frequency or phase.
ME	Meters	Multimeters, volt-ohm-milli-meters, vacuum tube voltmeters, power meters, etc.
MK	Miscellaneous kits	Maintenance, modification, etc.
ML	Meteorological devices	Miscellaneous meteorological equipment, etc.
MT	Mountings	Mountings, racks, frames, stands, etc.
MX	Miscellaneous	Equipment not otherwise classified. Do not use if better indicator is available.
MU	Memory units	Memory units.
O	Oscillators	Master frequency, blocking, multivibrators, etc. (for test oscillators, see SG).
OS	Oscilloscope, test	Test oscilloscope for general test purposes, (See IP).
PL	Plug-in units	Plug-in units not otherwise classified.
PP	Power supplies	Nonrotating machine type such as vibrator pack rectifier, thermoelectric, etc.
PT	Mapping and plotting units	Electronic types only.
PU	Power equipments	Rotating power equipment, motor generator, dynamotors, etc.
R	Receivers	Receivers, all types except telephone.
RD	Recorder - producers	Sound, graphic, tape, wire, film, disc, facsimile, magnetic, mechanical, etc.
RE	Relay assembly units	Electrical, electronic, etc.

RL	Reeling machines	Mechanism for dispensing and rewinding antenna or field wire, cable, etc.
RO	Recorders	Sound, graphic, tape, wire, film, disc, facsimile, magnetic, mechanical, tape and card punch, etc.
RP	Reproducers	Sound, graphic, tape, wire, film, disc, facsimile, magnetic, mechanical, punched tape and card readers, etc.
RR	Reflectors	Target, confusion, etc. Except antenna reflectors (See AS).
RT	Receiver and Transmitter	Radio and radar transceiver, composite transmitter and receiver, etc.
S	Shelter	Protective shelter, etc.
SA	Switching units	Manual, impact, motor driven, pressure operated, electronic, etc.
SB	Switchboards	Telephone, fire control, power, power distribution, etc.
SG	Generator, signal	Test oscillators, noise generators, etc. (See O).
SM	Simulators	Flight, aircraft, target, signal, etc.
SN	Synchronizers	Equipment to coordinate two or more functions.
SU	Optical units	Electro-optical units, such as, night vision, auto-collimator, scope, sights, viewers, trackers, alignment equipment.
T	Transmitters	Transmitters, all types, except telephone.
TA	Telephone apparatus	Miscellaneous telephone equipment.

TB	Towed body	Hydrodynamic enclosures used to house transducers, hydrophones, and other electronic equipment.
TD	Timing devices	Mechanical and electronic timing devices, range devices, multiplexers, electronic gates, etc.
TF	Transformers	When used as separate units.
TG	Positioning devices	Tilt and/or train assemblies.
TH	Telegraph apparatus	Miscellaneous telegraph apparatus.
TN	Tuning units	Receiver, transmitter, antenna, tuning units, etc.
TR	Transducers	Sonar transducers, vibration pickups, etc. (See H, LS, and M).
TS	Test units	Test and measuring equipment not otherwise classified. Do not use if more specific indicators apply.
TT	Teletypewriter and facsimile apparatus	Miscellaneous tape, teletype, facsimile equipment, etc.
TW	Tape units	Preprogrammed with operational test and check out data.
V	Vehicles	Carts, dollies, vans peculiar to electronic equipment.
ZM	Impedance measuring devices	Used for measuring Q, C, L, R, or PF, etc.

DEPARTMENT OF DEFENSE
DEFENSE LOGISTICS AGENCY

SALE 41-9183

BID OPENING:

27 APRIL   - 9:00 A.M.

SEALED BID

Offering... # ELECTRICAL AND ELECTRONIC COMPONENTS

Sample cover of U.S. Government Catalog

For Sale Site & Mailing Address See Page 59

FOR FURTHER INFORMATION SEE INSIDE

CHAPTER 11

GOVERNMENT SURPLUS DONATION PROGRAMS

Federal surplus donation programs enable certain non-Federal organizations to obtain personal property that the Federal Government no longer needs.

TYPES OF SURPLUS DONATED

The type of surplus that may be available under this program includes hand and machine tools, office machines and supplies, furniture, hardware, motor vehicles, boats, airplanes, construction equipment and many other items.

HOW DONABLE FEDERAL SURPLUS IS DISTRIBUTED

Each state, the District of Columbia, Puerto Rico, Virgin Islands and Guam have agencies established to distribute surplus property. Representatives of the state agencies visit U.S. Government installations to select property that is available for donation and they are notified by the General Services Administration of property that is available.

WHO IS ELIGIBLE TO RECEIVE DONATED GOVERNMENT SURPLUS?

Public Agencies

Public agencies involved in such activities as conservation, economic development, education, park programs and recreation, public safety, and public health may be eligible for donation of surplus personal property. Public agencies may include:
1. States, their departments, divisions, and other instrumentalities.
2. Political subdivisions of States, including cities, counties, and other local government units and economic-development districts.
3. Instrumentalities created by compacts or agreements between States or political subdivisions.
4. Indian tribes, bands, groups, pueblos, or communities located on State reservations.

Nonprofit Educational and Public Health Activities

Surplus personal property may be donated to nonprofit educational and public health activities exempt from taxation under Section 501 of the Internal Revenue Code of 1954. The property must be used to aid education or public health, either directly or through research. Nonprofit educational and public health activities may include:

1. Medical institutions, hospitals, clinics and health centers.
2. Schools, colleges, and universities.
3. Child-care centers.
4. Educational radio and TV stations.
5. Museums.
5. Libraries.

Educational Activities of Special Interest to the Armed Services

The Secretary of Defense has designated activities such as military and maritime academies, armed services preparatory schools, other schools with military-connected programs, and the national organizations listed below as recipients of Department of Defense surplus personal property:

1. American National Red Cross.
2. Boy Scouts of America.
3. Boys' Clubs of America
4. Camp Fire Girls.
5. Girl Scouts of the U.S.A.
6. Naval Sea Cadet Corps.
7. United Service Organizations, Inc.
8. Young Marines of the Marine Corps. League.

Individual units of the national organizations, such as Boy Scout or Girl Scout troops and Red Cross chapters, should contact their regional or national headquarters rather than the State surplus property agencies.

Public Airports

Any State, political subdivision, municipality, or tax-supported institution may receive surplus personal property through donation for use in the development, improvement, operation, or maintenance of a public airport.

FURTHER INFORMATION

The following offices may be contacted for general information that State surplus property offices are unable to supply.

All Eligible Groups:
Regional GSA offices or Office of Personal Property Disposal (FW)
 Federal Supply Service
 General Services Administration
 Washington, DC 20406

Armed-Services Educational Activities and National Organizations:
Assistant Secretary, Manpower, Reserve Affairs, and Logistics
Director, Precommissioning Programs
Department of Defense
The Pentagon
Washington, DC 20301

Public Airports:
Regional Federal Aviation Administration offices
(attn: Airports Branch Chief)
or
Office of Airport Programs
Federal Aviation Administration
Department of Transportation
Washington, DC 20591

STATE SURPLUS AGENCIES

Alabama
Alabama State Agency for
 Federal Property Assistance
P.O. Box 1100
Gadsden, AL 35902
(205) 492-6711

Alaska
Alaska Surplus Property Service
200 North Wrangell St.
Anchorage, AK 99501
(907) 279-0598

Arizona
Arizona Department of
  Administration
Surplus Property Division
5415 East Washington St.
Phoenix, AZ 85034
(602) 271-5701

Arkansas
Arkansas State Agency for
  Surplus Property
8700 Remount Rd.
North Little Rock, AR 72118
(501) 835-3111

California
California State Office of
  Federal Property
  Assistance
721 Capitol Mall
Sacramento, CA 95814
(916) 445-4943

Colorado
Colorado Surplus Property
  Agency
4700 Leetsdale Dr.
Denver, CO 80222
(303) 388-5953

Connecticut
Connecticut State Agency
  for Federal Surplus Property
60 State St.
P.O. Box 298
Wethersfield, CT 06109
(203) 529-8686

Delaware
Delaware Division of Purchasing
P.O. Box 299
Delaware City, DE 19706
(302) 834-4512

District of Columbia
General Services Administration
Bureau of Material
  Management
Surplus Acquisition Section
5 D.C. Village Lane, S.W.
Washington, D.C. 20032
(202) 629-8297

Florida
Florida Division of Surplus
  Property
Department of General Services
470 Larson Bldg.
Tallahassee, FL 32304
(904) 488-3524

Georgia
Georgia Agency for
  Federal Property Assistance
1050 Murphy Ave., SW
Atlanta, GA 30310
(404) 656-2681

Guam
Guam Department of
  Administration
Supply Management Division
P.O. Box 884
Agana, GU 96910
477-8836

Hawaii
Hawaii Department of
  Accounting and General
  Services
Surplus Property Branch
729 Kakoi St.
Honolulu, HI 96819
(808) 548-6946

Illinois
Illinois State Agency for
  Federal Surplus
  Property
4390 South Jeffory St.
Springfield, IL 62705
(217) 786-6940

Iowa
Iowa Surplus Property Section
Department of General
  Services
Grimes State Office Bldg.
Des Moines, IA 50319
(515) 281-5391

Kentucky
Kentucky Division of
  Surplus Property
Capitol Plaza Tower
Frankfort, KY 40601
(502) 564-4836

Maine
Maine State Agency of
  Surplus Property
Division of Community
  Services
State Office Bldg.
Augusta, ME 04333
(207) 289-2923

Idaho
Idaho Bureau of Surplus
  Property
P.O. Box 7414
Boise, ID 83707
(208) 384-3477

Indiana
Indiana State Agency for
  Federal Surplus
  Property
601 Kentucky Ave.
Indianapolis, IN 46225
(317) 633-5420

Kansas
Kansas Department of
  Administration
Surplus Property Section
R.R. 4, Box 36A
Topeka, KS 66603
(913) 296-2351

Louisiana
Louisiana Surplus Property
  Agency
Box 44351, Capitol Station
Baton Rouge, LA 70804
(504) 389-6571

Maryland
Maryland State Agency for
  Surplus Property
P.O. Box M
College Park, MD 20740
(301) 454-3910

Massachusetts
Massachusetts State
   Agency for
   Surplus Property
Park Square Bldg.
Room 502
31 St. James Ave.
Boston, MA 02116
(617) 727-5774

Minnesota
Minnesota Department of
   Administration
Materials Management
   Division
Federal Surplus Property
   Section
5420 Highway 8
New Brighton, MN 55112
(612) 633-1644

Missouri
Missouri State Agency for
   Surplus Property
117 North Riverside Dr.
P.O. Drawer 1310
Jefferson City, MO 65101
(314) 751-3415

Nebraska
Nebraska State Agency for
   Surplus Property
3321 North 35th St.
Lincoln, NE 68504
(402) 471-2495

Michigan
Michigan Department of
   Management and Budget
Office of Federal Property
   Assistance
3369 North Logan St.
P.O. Box 30026
Lansing, MI 48909
(517) 373-0560

Missippi
Mississippi Surplus
   Property Procurement
   Commission
Box 5778, Whitefield Rd.
Jackson, MS 39208
(601) 939-2050

Montana
Montana Office of Public
   Instruction
Division of Surplus Property
State Capitol Bldg.
Helena, MT 59601
(406) 449-2084

Nevada
Nevada Surplus Property
   Division
Nevada State Purchasing
Barnett Way
Reno, NV 89512
(702) 784-6408

New Hampshire
New Hampshire
   Distributing Agency
12 Hills Ave.
Concord, NH 03301
(603) 271-2602

New Mexico
New Mexico State Agency
   for Surplus Property
P.O. Box 4757 Coronado Station
Santa Fe, NM 87102
(505) 827-2511

North Carolina
North Carolina Federal
   Property Agency
P.O. Box 26567
Raleigh, NC 27611
(919) 733-3885

Ohio
Ohio State Agency for
   Surplus Property
   Utilization
4221 Westward Ave.
Columbus, OH 43228
(614) 466-4485

Oregon
Oregon Department of
   General Services
Purchasing Division
1225 Ferry Street, SE
Salem, OR 97310
(503) 379-4643

New Jersey
New Jersey State Agency for
   Surplus Property
Division of Civil Defense
P.O. Box 979
Trenton, NJ 08625
(609) 292-3862

New York
New York Bureau of
   Federal Property
   Assistance
Bldg. 18, Campus Site
Albany, NY 12226
(518) 457-3264

North Dakota
North Dakota Division of
   Surplus Property
State Capitol
Bismarck, ND 58505
(701) 224-2273

Oklahoma
Oklahoma State Agency
   for Surplus Property
P.O. Box 11355
Oklahoma City, OK 73111
(405) 521-2135

Pennsylvania
Pennsylvania Bureau of
   Surplus Property
2221 Forster St.
P.O. Box 3361
Harrisburg, PA 17125
(717) 787-5940

Puerto Rico
Puerto Rico State Agency
  for Federal Property
  Assistance
General Services Administration
Purchase Services and
  Supply Area
G.P.O. Box 4112
San Juan, PR 00905
(809) 724-0083

Rhode Island
Rhode Island State Agency
  for Surplus Property
Division of Purchases
State Warehouse
P.O. Box 8268
Cranston, RI 02920
(401) 464-2081

South Carolina
South Carolina Surplus
  Property Procurement
Division of General Services
Boston Ave.
West Columbia, SC 29169
(803) 758-2626

South Dakota
South Dakota Federal
  Property Agency
20 Colorado Ave., SW
Huron, SD 57350
(605) 352-8751

Tennessee
Tennessee Department of
  General Services
Federal Property
  Utilization Division
6500 Centennial Blvd.
Nashville, TN 37209
(615) 741-1711

Texas
Texas Surplus Property Agency
2103 Ackerman Rd.
P.O. Box 8120
Wainwright Station
San Antonio, TX 78208
(512) 661-2381

Utah
Utah State Agency for
  Surplus Property
522 South 700 West St.
Salt Lake City, UT 84104
(801) 533-5885

Vermont
Vermont Central Surplus
  Property Agency
87½ Barre Street
Montpelier, VT 05602
(802) 828-2213

Virgin Islands
Virgin Islands State Agency
for Surplus Property
Department of Property
and Procurement
Division of Property
P.O. Box 1437
St. Thomas, VI 00801
(809) 774-0414

Virginia
Virginia Federal Property
Agency
Department of Purchases
and Supply
217 Governor St.
Richmond, VA 23209
(804) 786-3884

Washington
Washington Surplus
Property Section
6858 South 190th St.
Kent, WA 98031
(206) 872-6446

West Virginia
West Virginia State Agency
for Surplus Property
2700 Charles Ave.
Dunbar, WV 25064
(304) 348-3510

Wisconsin
Wisconsin Federal
Property Program
201 South Dickinson St.
P.O. Box 1585
Madison, WI 53701
(608) 266-7839

Wyoming
Wyoming Federal Surplus
Property Agency
100 East 8th Ave.
Cheyenne, WY 82001
(307) 777-7669

For additional information on acquiring surplus personal property, contact the Director, Personal Property Disposal, Federal Supply Service, in the GSA region serving your area.

Region 1: Connecticut, Maine, Massachusetts, New Hampshire, Rhode Island, Vermont
John W. McCormack Post
Office and Courthouse
BOSTON, MA 02109
(617) 223-2394

Region 2: New Jersey, New York, Puerto Rico, Virgin Islands
26 Federal Plaza
NEW YORK, NY 10007
(212) 264-2034

Region 3: Delaware, District of Columbia, Maryland, Pennsylvania, Virginia, West Virginia
7th and D Sts., SW
WASHINGTON, DC 20407
(202) 472-2051

Region 4: Alabama, Florida Georgia, Kentucky, Mississippi, North Carolina, South Carolina, Tennessee
1776 Peachtree St., NW
ATLANTA, GA 30309
(404) 257-4520

Region 5: Illinois, Indiana, Michigan, Minnesota, Ohio, Wisconsin
230 South Dearborn St.
CHICAGO, IL 60604
(312) 353-6060

Region 6: Iowa, Kansas, Missouri, Nebraska
1500 East Bannister Rd.
KANSAS CITY, MO 64131
(816) 926-7251

Region 7: Arkansas, Louisiana, New Mexico, Oklahoma, Texas
819 Taylor St.
FORT WORTH, TX 76102
(817) 334-2330

Region 8: Colorado, Montana, North Dakota, South Dakota, Utah, Wyoming
Denver Federal Center
Bldg. 41
DENVER, CO 80225
(303) 234-5283

Region 9: American Samoa, Arizona, California, Guam, Hawaii, Nevada
525 Market St.
SAN FRANCISCO, CA 94105
(415) 556-3622

Region 10: Alaska, Idaho, Oregon, Washington
GSA Center
AUBURN, WA 98002
(206) 396-5388

CHAPTER 12

UNITED STATES CUSTOMS SERVICE AUCTIONS

Auctions of unclaimed items are held at each customs district office. In order to determine when sales will be held at the various locations, you should write to the District Director, U.S. Customs of the districts listed below.

Anchorage, Alaska 99501 / 204 E. Fifth Ave.

Baltimore, Maryland 21202 / 103 S. Gay St.
Boston, Massachusetts 02109 / 2 India St.
Bridgeport, Connecticut 06609 / 120 Middle St.
Buffalo, New York 14202 / 111 W. Huron St.

Charleston, South Carolina 29402 / 200 E. Bay St.
Chicago, Illinois 60607 / 610 S. Canal St.
Cleveland, Ohio 44114 / 55 Erieview Plaza

Detroit, Michigan 48226 / 477 Michigan Ave.
Duluth, Minnesota 55802 / 515 W. First St., 209 Fed. Bldg.

El Paso, Texas 79985 / Bldg. B, Room 134
    Bridge of the Americas (PO Box 9516)

Galveston, Texas 77550 / PO Bldg. (POB 570)
Great Falls, Montana 59401 / 215 1st Ave., N.

Honolulu, Hawaii 96806 / 335 Merchant St.
Houston, Texas 77052 / 701 San Jacinto St.

Laredo, Texas 78040 / Mann Rd. & Santa Maria (POB 758)
Los Angeles / Long Beach / 300 S. Ferry St.
    Terminal Island, San Pedro 90731

Miami, Florida 33131 / 77 S.E. 5th St.
Milwaukee, Wisconsin 53202 / 628 E. Michigan St.
Minneapolis, Minnesota 55401 / 110 S. Fourth St.
Mobile, Alabama 36602 / 250 N. Water St.

New Orleans, Louisiana 70130 / 600 South St.

New York, New York
  New York Seaport Area, New York, New York 10048
    Customhouse, 6 World Trade Center
  Kennedy Airport Area, Jamaica, New York 11430
    Seaboard World Building, Room 178
  Newark Area, Newark, New Jersey 07114
    Airport International Plaza
Nogales, Arizona 85621 / International & Terrace Sts.
Norfolk, Virginia 23510 / 101 E. Main St.

Ogdensburg, New York 13669 / 127 N. Water St.

Pembina, North Dakota 58271 / Post Office Bldg.
Philadelphia, Pennsylvania 19106 / 2nd & Chestnut Sts.
Port Authur, Texas 77640 / 5th & Austin Ave.
Portland, Maine 04111 / 312 Fore St.
Portland, Oregon 97209 / N.W. Broadway & Glisan Sts.
Providence, Rhode Island 02903 / 24 Weybosset St.

St. Albans, Vermont 05478 / Main & Stebbins St. (POB 111)
St. Louis, Missouri 63105 / 120 S. Central Ave.
St. Thomas, Virgin Islands 00801 / (POB 510)
San Diego, California 92188 / 880 Front St.
San Francisco, California 94126 / 555 Battery St. (POB 2450)
San Juan, Puerto Rico 00903 / (POB 2112)
Savanah, Georgia 31401 / 1 East Bay St.
Seattle, Washington 98174 / 909 First Ave.

Tampa, Florida 33602 / 301 S. Ashley Dr.

Washington, D.C. 20018 / 3180 Bladensburg Rd., N.E.
Wilmington, North Carolina 28401 / 2094 Polk St.

CHAPTER 13

UNITED STATES POSTAL SERVICE AUCTIONS

Auctions of unclaimed loose-in-the-mails items are held at least twice each year at each dead parcel branch. The scheduling and announcement of these sales is delegated to the mangagers of the various bulk mail centers where dead parcel branches are located. In order to determine when sales will be held at the various locations, you should write to the United States Post Office, General Manager of the Dead Parcel Branch listed below.

Atlanta, GA 30304
Chicago, IL 60607
Cincinnatti, OH 45234
Fort Worth, TX 76101
Denver, CO 80202
St. Paul, MN 55101
Detroit, MI 48233
Greensboro, NC 27420
Jacksonville, FL 32201
St. Louis, MO 63155

Los Angeles, CA 90052
Memphis, TN 38101
New York, NY 10001
Philadelphia, PA 19104
Pittsburgh, PA 15219
San Francisco, CA 94101
Seattle, WA 98109
Boston, MA 02109
Washington, D.C. 20013

DEPARTMENT OF DEFENSE

DEFENSE LOGISTICS AGENCY

SALE 41-9404

BID OPENING:

26 SEPTEMBER   **9:00 AM**

SEALED BID

Offering...

CONSTRUCTION & BUILDING MATERIALS

For Sale Site & Mailing

Address See Page 5

FOR FURTHER INFORMATION SEE INSIDE

CHAPTER 14

BUYING SURPLUS PROPERTY FROM
THE CANADIAN GOVERNMENT

There are six regional sales offices which sell Canadian Government surplus property. This surplus includes many of the items listed in Chapter 16.

If you wish to bid on items offered for sale through any of the six regional sales offices, you may do so by writing to each sales region in which you are interested.

Pacific Region, 4050 West 4th Ave., Vancouver, B.C., V6R 1P7
Prairie Region, 10645 Jasper Ave., Edmonton, Alberta, T5J 2A1
Ontario Region, 1191 Cawthra Rd., Mississauga, Ontario, L5G 4K8
National Capital Region, 25 Bentley Ave., P.O. Box 8750,
     Ottawa, Ontario, K1G 3J1
Quebec Region, 300 Notre-Dame St., Ville St-Pierre,
     Quebec, H8R 3Z6
Atlantic Region, 2 Morris Dr., Dartmouth, Nova Scotia, B3B 1K8

You may also write to the head office which co-ordinates all six sales regions at Crown Assets Disposal Corp., P.O. Box 8451, Ottawa, Ontario, Canada, K1G3J8.

Tell them you want to be put on the mailing list and to be notified of future sales of surplus material. Indicate the type of material in which you are interested and the region from which you wish to purchase. When material designated on your application is put on sale in your area, you will be sent an "Invitation to Bid" form which will contain detailed information regarding the location of the material, its description, condition, quantity, inspection dates, time and date of bid opening, payment and removal information.

The Canadian Government presently sells surplus material by the following methods:

Sealed Bid

The general method of "sealed bid" sales is described in Chapter 6.

Public Auction

The general method of "auction" is described in Chapter 6.

Retail Cash and Carry Sale

The general method of "retail" sales is described in Chapter 6.

Who May Not Bid on Canadian Government Surplus Material

1. Those under 18 years of age.
2. An employee of Crown Assets Disposal Corporation.
3. A member of the Canadian House of Commons.

CHAPTER 15

PACKAGING AND SHIPPING

Common carrier and packing companies will package and ship any item according to instructions, even prepare for exporting. Write and ask them to quote a price for packaging and/or shipping. For complete lists of companies that will make arrangements to pack, ship and crate the items purchased, subscribe to one of the many publications listing the origins and destinations served by common carriers. Listed below are the names and addresses of two of these firms.

National Highway Carriers Directory, Inc.,
936 South Betty Drive, P.O. Box U,
Buffalo Grove, Illinois 60090

Official Shippers Guide Company,
1130 South Canal Street,
Chicago, Illinois 60607

The following is a list of many of the defense property disposal offices and the packers, shippers and craters that have served customers at these facilities in the past.

The disposal offices are arranged by state and the services offered by these companies are indicated by the following legend. (C) Crating; (F) Freight; (H) Equipped to move heavy equipment; (P) Packing; (V) Equipped to move vehicles; (W) Water transportation; (I) Inspection.

ALABAMA

DPDO Anniston, Anniston, Alabama 36201
Howard Hall Co., Inc.,
    703 Clydesdale Ave., Anniston, AL 36201 (F, V, H, W)
Angle & Sons, Inc.,
    500 W. 22nd St., Anniston, AL 36201 (P, C, F)

DPDO Huntsville, Redstone Arsenal, Huntsville, AL 35809
Huntsville Van & Storage, Inc.,
    315 Jefferson St., N., Huntsville, AL 35801 (P, C, F, V, H)

DPDO Montgomery, Bldg. 900, Gunter AFS,
    Montgomery, AL 36114
Aero Mayflower Transit Co.,
    250 Commerce St., Montgomery, AL 36104 (P, C, W)
Bowman Transportation, Inc.,
    P.O. Box 2639, Montgomery, AL 36105 (F, V, H, W)

DPDO Rucker, Fort Rucker, Ozark, AL 36362
Gundy's Transfer Moving & Storage
    P.O. Box 1333, Enterprise, AL 36330 (P, C, F)

ALASKA

DPDO Anchorage, Anchorage P.O. Box 866, Elemendorf AFB,
    Anchorage, AK 99506
M.J.W. Service,
    P.O. Box 217, Clearfield, Utah 84015 (F, C, P, I)

DPDO Fairbanks, Fort Wainwright, Fairbanks, AK 99701
I.M.L. Freight Inc.,
    6024 S. College, Ft. Collins, Colorado 80521 (F)

ARIZONA

DPDO Luke, Luke A.F.B., Glendale, Arizona 85309
I.M.L. Freight Inc.,
    2175 S. 3270 W., Salt Lake City, Utah 84119 (F, C, P, I)

DPDO Tuscon, Davis-Monthan AFB, Tuscon, Arizona 85708
Time D.C.
    2943 E. Wieding Rd., Tucson, Arizona 85706 (F)

ARKANSAS

DPDO Blytheville AFB, Blytheville, ARK 73215
Arkansas-Best Freight System,
    P.O. Box 2428, Jonesboro, ARK 72401 (F)
Branscum Moving & Storage,
    812 North 6th, Blytheville, ARK 72315 (P, C)

DPDO Fort Chaffee, Fort Smith, ARK 72905
Ft. Smith Bonded Whse.,
    5320 S. 28th, Ft. Smith, ARK 72901 (P, C, F)
Rainwater Trucking Co.,
    1123 South 6th St., Ft. Smith, ARK 72901 (H)

DPDO Little Rock, Little Rock AFB, Jacksonville, ARK 72076
Briggs Bros. Van Lines,
    1127 Stagecoach Rd., Little Rock, ARK 72206 (P, C, F, V)
McConnell Heavy Hauling, Inc.,
    Highway 365 South, Little Rock, ARK 72206 (F, V, H)

DPDO Pine Bluff Arsenal, Pine Bluff, ARK 71601
ABF (Arkansas Best Freight)
    Rt. 4, Box 106-B, Pine Bluff, ARK 71601 (F, V, H)
Aero Mayflower World Wide,
    P.O. Box 8269, Pine Bluff, ARK 71601 (P, C)

CALIFORNIA

**DPDO Alameda, Bldg. 6, 2155 Mariner Square Loop,
    Alameda, Calif. 94501**
Capitol Surplus Expediters,
    P.O. Box 7281, 5121 Hedge Ave.,
    Sacramento, Calif. 95826 (F, C, P, I)
Western Gillette Inc.,
    601 W. Flores, Tucson, Arizona 85705 (F)

DPDO Barstow, Marine Corps. Logistics Support Base Pacific, Barstow, Calif. 92311
Barstow Truck Lines,
  1550 State St., Barstow, Calif. 92311 (F, C, P, I)

DPDO El Toro, P.O. Box 21, East Irvine, Calif. 92650
IML Freight Inc.,
  2175 S. 3270 W., Salt Lake City, Utah 84119 (F, C, P, I)

DPDO McClellan, McClellan AFB, Sacramento, Calif. 95652
IML Freight Inc.,
  2175 S. 3270 W., Salt Lake City, Utah 84119 (F, C, P, I)

DPDO Norton, Norton AFB, San Bernardino, Calif. 92409
Victorville Barstow Truck Lines, 1550 State St.,
  Barstow, Calif. 92311 (F, C, P, I)

DPDO—ORD, Fort Ord, Monterey, Calif. 93941
Consolidated Freightways,
  4723 W. Hacienda, Las Vegas, Nevada 89103 (F)
IML Freight Inc.,
  2175 S. 3270 W., Salt Lake City, Utah 84119 (F, C, P, I)

DPDO Camp Pendleton, P.O. Box 1608, Oceanside, Calif. 92054
IML Freight Inc.,
  2175 S. 3270 W., Salt Lake City, Utah 84119 (F, C, P, I)

DPDO Port Hueneme, Naval Construction BN Center, Port Hueneme, Calif. 93043
Navajo Freight Lines,
  4575 Tidewater, Oakland, Calif. 94601 (F)

DPDA, Naval Station Scrapyard, National City, Calif. 92050
IML Freight Inc.,
  2175 S. 3270 W., Salt Lake City, Utah 84119 (F, C, P, I)

DPDO Stockton, Bldg. 1002, Rough and Ready Island,
    Stockton, Calif. 95203
Packfic Storage Co.,
    734 Wilshire Ave., P.O. Box 334,
    Stockton, Calif. 95201 (F, C, P, I)

DPDO Vandenberg, P.O. Box 1685, Vandenberg AFB,
    Lompoc, Calif. 93437
Smith Transportation Co.,
    731 S. Lincoln St., P.O. Box 1259,
    Santa Maria, Calif. 93454 (F)

COLORADO

DPDO Colorado Springs, Fort Carson, Colorado Springs, CO 80913
Time D.C.,
    3888 E. 45th Ave., Denver, CO 80216 (F, I)

CONNECTICUT

DPDO Groton, Box 12, Naval Submarine Base New London,
    Groton, Conn. 06340
Thames Moving Co., Inc.,
    563 Colman St., New London, Conn. 06320 (P, C, F)

DELAWARE

DPDO Dover, DE, Bldg. 114, Dover AFB, DE 19901
Rea Express,
    McKee Rd., Dover, DE 19901 (F)
Scott Moving & Storage,
    Lynch Heights, Milford DE 19963 (P, C)

FLORIDA

DPDHA Cape Canaveral Air Force Station,
    Cape Canaveral, FLA 32920
Cape Can. Moving & Storage,
    515 W. Baron Ave., Rockledge FLA 32955 (P, C, F, V)

**DPDO Cecil Field, Naval Air Station - Cecil Field,
Jacksonville, FLA 32215**
Gillespie Moving & Storage,
P.O. Box 7642, Jacksonville, FLA 32205 (P, C, F, V, H, W)

DPDO Elgin AFB, Valparaiso, FLA 32542
Bonded Transportation Inc.,
P.O. Box 1529 Ft., Walton Bch., FLA 32548 (P, C, F, V, H)

DPDO Homestead, P.O. Box 1529, Homestead, FLA 33030
Bekins Moving & Storage Co.,
650 N.W. 105 St., Miami, FLA 33150 (P, C)
Suddath Van Lines Inc.,
275 North Canal Dr., Florida City, FLA 33030 (P, C, F)

DPDO Jacksonville Naval Air Station, Jacksonville, FLA 32212
Gillespie Moving & Storage,
P.O. Box 7642, Jacksonville, FLA 32205 (P, C, F, V, H, W)

DPDO Key West, NAS Truman Annex, Key West, FLA 33040
Overseas Transportation Co., Inc.,
1101 Eaton St., Key West, FLA 33040 (F, H)
Southern Enterprises, Inc.,
930 Catherine St., Key West, FLA 33040 (P, C)

DPDO Orlando, U.S. Naval Training Center, Orlando FLA 32813
Leonard Bros. Trucking Co.,
1411 S. Orange Blossom Tr., Orlando, FLA (P, C., F, V, H)

DPDO Patrick, Patrick AFB, Cocoa Beach, FLA 32925
Ward Moving & Storage Co.,
317 Clearlake Rd., Cocoa, FLA 32922 (P, C, F, V, H)

DPDO Pensacola, U.S. Naval Air Station, Pensacola, FLA 32508
Best Line Moving & Storage,
126 East Chase Street, Pensacola, FLA 32501 (P, C, F)

DPDO Tampa, Mac Dill AFB, Tampa, FLA 33608
American Red Ball, Vetzel Moving & Storage,
103 N. 12th St., Tampa, FLA 33602 (P, C, F, V, H, W)

DPDO Tyndall, Tyndall AFB, Panama City, FLA 32403
Allied Van Lines,
901 Mulberry Ave., Panama City, FLA 32401 (P, C, F)
Howard Hall,
722 N. Kraft Ave., Panama City, FLA 32401 (F, V, H)

GEORGIA

DPDO Albany, Marine Corp. Logistics Support Base Atlantic,
Albany, GA 31704
Newcomb, Inc.,
2400 N. Monroe St., Albany, GA 31701 (P, C, F)
Ryder Truck Lines, Inc.,
501 Maxwell Dr., Albany, GA 31705 (F, V, H)

DPDO Benning, P.O. Box 3760, Columbus, GA 31903
Delcher Moving & Storage,
2710 13th St., Phenix City, AL 36867 (P, C, F, V, H, W)

DPDO Dobbins, Dobbins AFB, GA 30060
Ryder Truck Lines, Inc.,
2300 Jonesboro Rd., S.E., Atlanta, GA 30315 (P, C, F, H)
Motor Convoy Inc.,
275 Convoy Dr., S.W., Atlanta, GA 30315 (V)

DPDO Forest Park, P.O. Box 1588, Forest Park, GA 30050
Acme Moving & Storage Co.,
1031 Lee St., S.W., Atlanta, GA 30310 (P, C)
Central Truck Lines,
1952 Moreland Ave., S.E., Atlanta, GA 30316 (F)
Moss Trucking Co.,
4780 Old Dixie Hwy, Forest Park, GA 30050 (V, H)

**DPDO Glynco NAS, Brunswick, GA Satellited on
Fort Stewart, Hinesville, GA 31313**
Akers Motor Lines, Inc.,
    32 Dixie Ave., Brunswick, GA 31520 (F, V)
Benton Brothers, Drayage & Storage Co.,
    3120 Hopkins Ave., Brunswick, GA 31520 (P, C, F)

DPDO Gordon, Fort Gordon, Augusta, GA 30905
H & S Transfer Co.,
    1240 Gordon Park Rd., Augusta, GA 30901 (P, C, F, V, H)

DPDO Stewart, P.O. Box 85, Hinesville, GA 31313
Suddath of Savannah,
    5003 Liberty Parkway, Savannah, GA 31402 (P, C, F, W)
Thurston Motor Lines, Inc.,
    802 Hwy 80 W., Savannah, GA 31401 (F, V, H)

DPDO Valdosta, Moody AFB, Valdosta, GA 31601
Terminal Transport Co.,
    Conoly Ave., Valdosta, GA 31601 (F)
Ortlieb Moving & Storage Co.,
    W. Savannah Ave., Valdosta, GA 31601 (P, C)

DPDO Warner Robins, Robins AFB, Warner Robins, GA 31098
D.S.S.M.C. Agency,
    155 Columbia Rd., P.O. Box 212, Parnassus Station,
    New Kensington, PA 15068 (P, C, F, V, H)

ILLINOIS

DPDO Chanute, Bldg. 734, Chanute AFB, Rantoul, ILL 61868
Johnson's Moving & Storage,
    221 S. Maplewood, Rantoul, ILL 61866 (P, F)

**DPDO Great Lakes, Naval Training Center, Bldg. 3212A,
Great Lakes, ILL 60088**
Kenneth Narrod Moving Co.,
1515 Morrow, North Chicago, ILL 60064 (P, C)
Hennis Freight Lines, Inc.,
7700 S. Cicero Ave., Chicago, ILL 60652 (F, C)

**DPDO Joliet, Army Ammunition Plant, P.O. Box 871,
Joliet, ILL 60434**
Joliet Warehouse & Transfer,
12 New St., Joliet, ILL 60434 (P, F)

**DPDO Rock Island, Rock Island Arsenal, Bldg. 145,
Rock Island, ILL 61299**
Yellow Freight Systems Inc.,
3815 W. River Dr., Davenport, Iowa (F)
Voss Bros, Express & Storage,
2125 3rd Ave., Rock Island, ILL (P)

DPDO Savanna, Savanna Army Depot, Savanna, ILL 61074
Bill's Moving & Storage,
2640 46th Ave., Rock Island, ILL 61201 (P, C, F)

DPDO Scott, Scott AFB, Belleville, ILL 62225
Laquet Motor Service,
315 Hanna St., Mascoutah, ILL 62258 (F)
Robert J. Gooding,
801 Scheel St., Belleville, ILL 62221 (P, C)

INDIANA

DPDO Crane, Naval Weapons Support Center, Crane, IND 47522
Henderson Transfer Co., Inc.,
1611 Broadway St., Vincennes, IND 47591 (F, P)
R. L. Jeffries Trucking Co.,
1020 Pennsylvania Ave., Evensville, IND 47731 (F, H)

71

DPDO Grissom, Grissom AFB, Peru, Indiana 46971
Guyer the Mover,
    304 E. 6th St., Peru, IND 46970 (P, C, F)

DPDO Indiana Army Ammunition Plant, Charlestown, IND 47111
Wrights Moving & Storage, Inc.,
    1115 Vincennes St., New Albany, IND 47150 (P, C)

DPDO Indianapolis, P.O. Box 16307,
    Fort Benjamin Harrison, IND 46216
Art Poe's Moving & Storage,
    3833 Prospect, Indianapolis, IND 46203 (F, P)

DPDO Jefferson Proving Ground, Madison, IND 47250
OK Trucking Co.,
    1145 Cliffty Dr., Madison, IND 47250 (F)

DPDO Newport Army Ammunition Plant, P.O. Box 121,
    Newport, IND 47966
I & S McDaniel, Inc.,
    201 N. First St., Terre Haute, IND 47807 (F, P)

IOWA

DPDO Iowa Army Ammunition Plant, Middletown, Iowa 52638
Consolidated Freightways,
    105 S. Roosevelt, Burlington, IA 52601 (F)
Atlas Warehouse Co.,
    923 Osborn St., Burlington, IA 52601 (P, C)

KANSAS

Defense Industrial Plant Equip. Facility, Atchison, KS 66002
Catitoc Truck Lines, Inc.,
    2nd & Commercial, Atchison, KS

Kansas Army Ammunition Plant, Parsons, Kansas 67357
Reynolds Transfer & Storage Co.,
604 Main St., Parsons, KS 67357 (P, C)
Wichita Southeast Kansas Transit,
207 S. 32nd, Parsons, KS 67357 (F)

DPDO Leavenworth, Bldg. 269, Fort Leavenworth, KS 66027
Studdart Transfer & Storage Co.,
782 Seneca St., Leavenworth KS 66048 (F, P)

DPDO McConnell, McConnell AFB, Wichita, KS 67221
Pad Bloc Co.,
P.O. Box 213, Wichita, KS 67201 (P, C, F)

DPDO Riley, P.O. Box 2490, Fort Riley, KS 66442
Coleman Transfer & Storage,
615 S. 11th, Manhattan, KS 66502 (P, C, F)

Sunflower Army Ammunition Plant - Lawrence, KS 66044
Lawrence Freight Line, Inc.,
1521 North Third, Lawrence, KS 66044 (F, P, C)

KENTUCKY

DPDO Campbell, P.O. Box 555, Fort Campbell,
    Hopkinsville, KY 42223
Marvin Hayes Truck Lines,
P.O. Box 68, Clarksville, TN 37040 (P, C, F)
Illinois Central Gulf Railroad,
Spring St., Clarksville, TN 37040 (F, V, H)

DPDO Knox, Fort Knox, KY 40121
Arco Auto Carriers,
Galion, OH 44833 (V)
D.S.S.M.C. Agency,
155 Columbia Rd., P.O. Box 212, Parnassus Station,
New Kensington, PA 15068 (P, C, F)

DPDO Lexington, Lexington Blue Grass Army Depot Activity, Lexington, KY 40511
Vincent Fister, Inc.,
2305 Palumbo Dr., Lexington, KY 40509 (P, C, F)

DPDO Lexington - Blue Grass Army Depot, Richmond, KY 40475
Bronaugh Motor Express, Inc.,
1025 Nandino Blvd., Lexington, KY 40511 (F)

DPDO U.S. Naval Ordnance Station, Louisville, KY 40214
Grovers Moving & Storage,
506 E. Caldwell, Louisville, KY 40203 (P, C)
George Transfer & Rigging Co.,
2808 7th St. Rd., Louisville, KY 40215 (C, F)

LOUISIANA

DPDO England, England AFB, Alexandria, LA 71301
Hathorn Transfer & Storage Co.,
620 Elliot, Alexandria, LA 71301 (P, C, F, V)

DPDO Barksdale, Barksdale AFB, Shreveport LA 71110
Ryder Truck Lines, Inc.,
1320 Airport Dr., P.O. Box 87,
Shreveport, LA 71102 (F, V, H)
Central Storage & Transfer Co., Inc.,
1635 Texas Ave., P.O. Box 1778,
Shreveport, LA 71166 (P, C, F)

DPDO Polk, Fort Polk, Leesville, LA 71459
C & H Transportation Co.,
    Farm Rd. 250 N., Lone Star, TX 75668 (V, H)
McLean Trucking Company,
    4010 Goodman Lane, Lake Charles, LA 70601 (F)

MAINE

DPDO Brunswick, Naval Air Station, Brunswick, Maine 04011
Bisson Moving & Storage,
    New Meadows Rd., W. Bath, Maine 04530 (P, C)

DPDO Limestone, Loring AFB, Maine 04751
Parker K. Bailey & Sons,
    Houlton Rd., Presque Isle, Maine (P, C)

MARYLAND

DPDO Aberdeen, Aberdeen Proving Ground, Aberdeen, MD 21005
Associated Transport Inc.,
    2101 Washington Blvd., Baltimore, MD 21230 (F)
Park Moving & Crating,
    Aberdeen, MD 21001 (P, C, F)

DPDO Brandywine, P.O. Box 147, Brandywine, MD 20613
Merchants Transfer & Storage Co.,
    1616 1st St., S.W., Washington, D.C. (F, P, C)

DPDO Meade, Fort Meade, MD 20755
Aarid Van Lines,
    1337 S. Hanover St., Baltimore, MD 21230 (P, C, F)

DPDHA Naval Air Station, Patuxent River, MD 20670
Preston Trucking Company,
    151 Blades La, Glen Burnie, MD 21061 (F)

U.S. Coast Guard Yard, Curtis Bay, Baltimore, MD 21226
Arrid Consolidated Service,
   1335 S. Hanover St., Baltimore, MD 21201 (P, C, F)

U.S. Naval Academy, Annapolis, MD 21402
American Transfer Co.,
   112 Race St., Baltimore, MD (F)

MASSACHUSETTS

DPDO Ayer, Fort Devens, P.O. Drawer D, Ayer, MASS 01432
A.C.E. Freight, Inc.,
   28 Travis, Allston, MASS (F)

**DPDO Chicopee Falls, Bldg. 1604 Westover AFB,
   Chicopee Falls, MASS 01022**
Spector Freight System, Inc.,
   New Lombard Rd., Chicopee Falls, MASS 01020 (F)
Central Storage Warehouse, Inc.,
   270 Liberty St., Springfield, MASS 01100 (P, C)

DPDO Otis, Bldg. 1747, Otis AFB, MASS 02542
Universal Carloading & Dist.,
   80 Western Ave., Boston, MA 02134 (F)
F. B. Rich & Sons, Inc.,
   Waquoit Village, Falmouth, MA 02540 (P, C)

MICHIGAN

DPDO Sawyer, Bldg. 417, K.I. Sawyer AFB, Mich. 49843
Frost Moving & Storage,
   U.S. 41 Hwy., Negaunee, Mich. 49866 (P,C)

DPDO Selfridge, Air National Guard, Mt. Clemons, Mich. 48041
D.S.S.M.C. Agency,
    155 Columbia Rd., P.O. Box 212, Parnassus Station,
    New Kensington, PA 15068 (F, P, C)

DPDO Detroit, USA Tarcom (MAMP) Bldg. 2, Warren, Mich. 48090
Short Freight Lines, Inc.,
    4200 Sharon Ave., Detroit, Mich. 48210 (F)
Quality Packing Systems,
    24240 Mound Rd., Warren, Mich. 48091 (P)

DPDO Wurtsmith, P.O. Box C, Wurtsmith AFB, Mich. 48753
D.S.S.M.C. Agency,
    155 Columbia Rd., P.O. Box 212, Parnassus Station,
    New Kensington, PA 15068 (P, F)

MINNESOTA

DPDO Duluth, Duluth International Airport, Duluth, MINN 55814
Admiral Merchants Transportation,
    3006 W. 1st St., Duluth, MINN 55807 (F)

Twin Cities Army Ammunition Plant, New Brighton, MINN 55112
Backdahl Uptown Transfer Co.,
    716 W. 26th St., Minneapolis, MINN 55405 (P, C, F)

MISSISSIPPI

DPDO Columbus, Columbus AFB, Columbus, MS 39701
Superior Trucking Co.,
    2770 Peyton Rd., Atlanta, GA 30321 (V, H)
Heatherly Moving & Storage,
    Box 2186 E. End Sta., Columbus, MS 39701 (P, C)

DPDO Keesler, Keesler AFB, Biloxi, MS 39534
Fayard Moving & Transportation Co.,
  2615 25th Ave., Gulfport, MS 39501 (P, C, F, V, H, W)

**DPDO U.S. Army Engineer Waterways Experiment Sta.,
  Vicksburg, MS 39180**
Arkansas Best Freight System, Inc.,
  P.O. Box 405, Vicksburg, MS 39180 (F)

MISSOURI

DPDHA Richards-Gebaur AFB, Grandview, MO 64030
Bekin Moving & Storage,
  3429 Troost Ave., Kansas City, MO 64116 (P, F)

Lake City Army Ammunition Plant, Independence, MO 64056
Lyon Moving & Storage,
  10415 Hickman Mills Dr., Hickman Mills, MO 64137 (P, C)
Byers Trans. Co.,
  4200 Gardner, Kansas City, MO 64120 (P, C)

DPDO Leonard Wood, Fort Leonard Wood, Waynesville, MO 65473
A-1 Moving & Storage,
  6th & Cedar Sts., Rolla, MO 65401 (P, C, F)

DPDO Whiteman, P.O. Box 6010, Whiteman AFB, MO 65305
A-1 Mid State Storage, Inc.,
  118 N. Lamine, Sedalia, MO 65301 (P, F)

MONTANA

**DPDO Great Falls, P.O. Box 7001, Malstrom AFB,
  Great Falls, Montana 59402**
Consolidated Freightways,
  305 6th St., NW, Great Falls, Montana 59404 (F)

NEBRASKA

**Cornhusker Army Ammunition Plant, P.O. Box 2041,
Grand Island, NE 68801**
Arrow Freight Line,
    E. Highway 30, Grand Island NE 68801 (P, C, F)

DPDO Offutt AFB, P.O. Box 13292, Omaha, NE 68113
I-GO Van & Storage Co.,
    7601 Dodge, Omaha, NE 68114 (P, C, F)

NEVADA

DPDO Nellis, Nellis AFB, Las Vegas, NEV 89191
IML Freight Inc.,
    2175 S. 3270 W., Salt Lake City, Utah 84119 (F, C, P, I)

NEW HAMPSHIRE

**DPDO Portsmouth, Portsmouth Naval Shipyard, P.O. Box 2028,
Portsmouth, N.H. 03801**
McLean Trucking,
    Elms St., Biddeford, ME 04005 (P, F)

NEW JERSEY

**DPDO Bayonne, Military Ocean Terminal, Bldg. 63,
Bayonne, N.J. 07002**
Treadway Express Inc.,
    Highway 33 & Probasco Rd., Heightstown, N.J. (F)
A. G. Rogers, Inc.,
    931 Asbury Ave., Asbury Park, N.J. (P, C)

DPDO Colts-Neck, Naval Weapons Station, Earle Bldg. C-33, Colts Neck, N.J. 07722
Treadway Express Inc.,
  Highway 33 & Probasco Rd., Heightstown, N.J. (F)
A. G. Rogers, Inc.,
  931 Asbury Ave., Asbury Park, N.J. (P, C)

DPDO Dover Picatinny Arsenal, Dover, N.J. 87801
Allied Van Lines,
  76 Sussex St., Dover, N.J. 07801 (P, C)
Cooper-Jarrett Truck Lines,
  250 N. Clinton St., Dover, N.J. 07801 (F)

DPDO Lakehurst, Naval Air Station Bldg. 75, Lakehurst, N.J. 08733
Asbury Neptune Truck Co.,
  1112 11th Ave., Neptune, N.J. 07753 (F)
Atlantic Moving Co.,
  51 Wood Ave., Brick Town, N.J. 08723 (P, C)

NEW MEXICO

DPDO Cannon, Cannon AFB, Clovis, NM 88101
ABC Moving & Storage,
  1009 E. 1st St., Clovis, NM 88101 (P, F)

DPDO Holloman AFB, Alamogordo, NM 88330
Navajo Freight Line, Inc.,
  2210 White Sands Blvd., Alamogordo, NM 88310 (F, V, H)
Apaca Moving & Storage,
  2701 Airport Rd., Alamogordo, NM 88310 (P, C)

DPDO Kirtland, Kirtland AFB, Albuquerque, NM 87117
Albuquerque Moving & Storage Co., Inc.,
  7510 Menaul Blvd. NE, Albuquerque, NM 87110 (P, C)
ICX-Illinois-California Express,
  P.O. Box 3788, Albuquerque, NM 87110 (F, V, H, W)

NEW YORK

DPDO Plattsburgh, Plattsburgh AFB, Plattsburgh, NY 12903
Homer Mayflower,
  Hammond La., Plattsburgh, NY 12901 (P, C)
Coolidge Movers, Inc.,
  Skyway Shopping Center, Plattsburgh, NY 12901 (F)

DPDO Rome, Bldg. T-8, Griffiss AFB, Rome, NY 13441
Modern Moving & Storage,
  Coleman Mills Rd., Rome, NY 13440 (P, F)

DPDHA Seneca Army Depot, Romulus, NY 14541
Tayntons Motor Freight,
  407 Third St., Ithaca, NY 14850 (F, P)

DPDO Watertown, Fort Drum, Watertown, NY 13601
DeLuxe Lines, Inc..
  424 Newell St., Watertown, NY 13601 (F)

**DPDO Watervliet, Watervliet Arsenal, Bldg. 145,
  Watervliet, NY 12189**
Navajo Freight Lines,
  144 Sticker Rd., Latham, NY (F)
Brukins & Foley,
  33 N. Lansing St., Albany, NY 12207 (P, C)

NORTH CAROLINA

**DPDO Bragg, Bldg. 8-T-3015, Macomb St., Ft. Bragg,
  Fayetteville, NC 28307**
ABC Transfer Co.,
  P.O. Box 341, 834 McDuffie St.,
  Fayettville, NC 28302 (P, C, F)

**DPDO Lejeune, Bldg. 906, Camp Lejeune,
    Jacksonville, NC 28542**
Weathers Brothers,
    P.O. Box 907, Jacksonville, NC 28540 (P, C)
International Transport Inc.,
    P.O. Box 448, New Kingston, PA 17072 (H)

DPDO MCAS, Cherry Point, P.O. Box 948, Havelock, NC 28532
Simmons Transfer Co., Inc.,
    P.O. Drawer G, Newport, NC 28570 (P, C, F)

DPDO Goldsboro, Seymour Johnson AFB, Goldsboro, NC 27531
Security Storage,
    Hwy, 117 By-Pass S., Goldsboro, NC 27530 (P, C, F)
Aaron Smith Trucking Co.,
    Dudley, NC (F, V, H)

NORTH DAKOTA

**DPDO Grand Forks, Grand Forks AFB, Bldg. 432,
    Grand Forks,North Dakota 58205**
Midwest Motor Express Inc.,
    Hwy. 81 N., Grand Forks, North Dakota 58201 (F)

DPDO Minot, Minot AFB, North Dakota 58705
Kedney Warehouse Co.,
    11 2nd St., NE, Minot, North Dakota 58701 (F, C, P, I)

OHIO

Defense Construction Supply Center, Columbus, OH 43213
Edwards Transfer & Storage,
    2170 Eakin Rd., Columbus, OH 43223 (F, H)
KAPAC Company,
    800 Curtis, Columbus, OH 43203 (P, C)

Ravenna Army Ammunition Plant, Ravenna, OH 44266
McVay Transfer & Storage Co.,
    2190 State Rt. 59, Ravenna, OH 44266 (P, F)

DPDO Wright Patterson, Bldg. 743, Area B,
    Wright Patterson AFB, OH 45433
Acme Burns Pack and Ship,
    1105 Printz Ave., Dayton, OH (F, C, P)

OKLAHOMA

DPDO Altus AFB, Altus, OK 73521
3-D Transportation Corp.,
    Box 743, Altus, OK 73521 (P, C, F, V, H)

DPDO Oklahoma City, Tinker AFB / L-11,
    Oklahoma City, OK 73145
Shirley Laws,
    Route 1, Box 110-R, Choctaw, OK 73020 (P, C, V, F, H)

DPDO McAlester, US Army Ammo Plant, McAlester, OK 74501
Johnson Transfer & Storage, Inc.,
    69 Bypass, S., McAlester, OK 74501 (P, C)
Little Dixie Xpress LTD,
    P.O. Box 95252, Oklahoma City, OK 73143 (V, H)

DPDO-SILL, Fort Sill, Lawton, OK 73503
O.K. Transfer & Storage,
    202 East D. St., Lawton, OK 73501 (P, C)
Yellow Transit,
    P.O. Box 2326, Wichita Falls, TX 76307 (F, V)

PENNSYLVANIA

DPDO Chambersburg, Letterkenny Army Depot, Chambersburg, PA 17201
H. C. Gabler,
 RD 3, Chambersburg, PA 17201 (F)
Chambersburg Waste Paper Co.,
 662 Lincoln Way West, Chambersburg, PA 17201 (P, C)

DPDO Mechanicsburg, Navy SPCC Mechanicsburg, Bldg. 206, Mechanicsburg, PA 17055
Harrisburg Storage Co.,
 2nd & Paxton Sts., Harrisburg, PA 17104 (P, C, F)

DPDO Philadelphia, Philadelphia Naval Base, Bldg. 648, Philadelphia, PA 19112
Transamerican Freight Line,
 3000 Orthodox, Philadelphia, PA (F)
Atlas Storage Co.,
 32nd & Jefferson, Philadelphia, PA (P, C)

DPDO Tobyhanna, P.O. Box 1000, Tobyhanna, PA 18466
Albert Yascavage,
 P.O. Box 215, Hunlock Creek, PA 18621 (P, C)

PUERTO RICO

DPDO Buchanan, Fort Buchanan, Puerto Rico, APO Miami 34040
Capital Transportation Inc.,
 P.O. Box 3008, San Juan, Puerto Rico 00939 (P, C, F, V, H, W)

RHODE ISLAND

**DPDO Davisville, Naval Construction Battalion Ctr.,
Davisville, RI 02854**
Hemingway Transport, Inc.,
   Amaral St., E. Providence, RI 02914 (F, P, C)
George Arpin & Sons, Inc.,
   85 Carlsbad St., Cranston, RI (P, C, F)

**DPDO Newport, Naval Education Training Center,
Newport, RI 02840**
Adley Express Co., Inc.,
   1370 Elmwood Ave., Cranston, RI (F, P)
Hallamore, Inc.,
   Plymouth Rd., Holbrook, MA (F, H)

DPDSA, P.O. Box 100, Portsmouth, RI 02871
George Arpin & Sons Inc.,
   85 Carlsbad St., Cranston, RI (P, C, F)

SOUTH CAROLINA

**DPDO Charleston, Naval Supply Center,
North Charleston, SC 29406**
Palmetto Moving & Storage Inc.,
   P.O. Box 4055, Charleston Hgts., SC 29405 (P, C, F, V, H)

**DPDO Jackson, Bldg. 1902, Fort Jackson,
Columbia, SC 29207**
Tisdale Transfer & Storage,
   1921 Edmund Hwy., Cayce, SC 29022 (P, C)
C & H Transportation Co.,
   Rt. 378, W. Columbia, SC 29169 (V, H)

DPDO Myrtle Beach AFB, Myrtle Beach, SC 29577
Chavis Van & Storage,
     P.O. Box 1616, Myrtle Beach, SC 29577 (P, C, F, V, H)

DPDO Parris Island, Marine Corps. Recruit Depot, P.O. Box 5164 Parris Island, SC 29905
Carolina Moving & Storage Co.,
     P.O. Box 964, Beaufort, SC 29902 (P, C, F)

DPDO Fort Jackson, Columbia, SC 29207
Rowland Bros. Moving & Storage,
     17 Commerce St., Sumter, SC 29150 (P, C)
Allied Van Lines,
     1429 N. Main St., Sumter, SC 29150 (F)
C & H Transportation Co.,
     Rt. 378, W. Columbia, SC 29169 (V, H)

SOUTH DAKOTA

DPDO Ellsworth, Ellsworth AFB, Rapid City, South Dakota 57706
Consolidated Freightways,
     4723 W. Hacienda, Las Vegas, NEV 89103 (F)

TENNESSEE

DPDO Holston Army Ammunition Plant, Kingsport, TN 37662
Associated Transport, Inc.,
     Kingsport, TN 37660 (F)

DPDO Memphis, 2163 Airways Blvd., Memphis, TN 38114
Rock Island Lines,
     700 S. 5th, Memphis, TN 38126 (F, V, H)
J. A. Shelton Transfer Co.,
     3157 Bellbrook Center Dr. E., Memphis TN 38116 (P, C, F)

DPDO Naval Air Station, Millington, TN 38054
Bowman Transportation, Inc.,
    461 Winchester Rd., Memphis, TN 38105 (F)

Volunteer Army Ammo Plant, Chattanooga, TN 37401
Arrow Transfer & Storage Co.,
    1130 Market St., Chattanooga, TN (F)

TEXAS

DPDO Bergstrom AFB, Austin, TX 78743
Austin Fireproof Storage & Moving Co.,
    3201 Longhorn Blvd., Austin TX 78758 (P, C, F, V, H)

DPDO Carswell, P.O. Box 27177, Carswell AFB,
    Fort Worth, TX 76127
Bekins Van Lines,
    3209 Alta Mere, Ft. Worth, TX 76106 (P, C, F, V, W)
Active Moving & Storage,
    5110 Rondo Dr., Ft. Worth, TX 76106 (P, C, V, H, W)

DPDO Corpus Christi, Bldg. 22, Naval Air Station,
    Corpus Christi, TX 78419
MAC Transfer & Storage,
    622 Powers, Corpus Christi, TX 78401 (P, C, F, V)
Southwestern Motor Transport, Inc.,
    350 McCampbell, Corpus Christi, TX 78410 (F, V, H)

DPDO Fort Bliss, P.O. Box 8029, El Paso, TX 79908
Lee Way Motor Freight, Inc.,
    1005 Tony Lama St., El Paso, TX 79915 (F, V, H)
Bond Transfer, Inc.,
    1831 Mills, El Paso, TX 79901 (P, C)

DPDO Hood, P.O. Drawer G, Fort Hood, Killeen, TX 76544
Towne Services,
>3101 E. Highway 190, Killeen, TX 76541 (P, C, F)

DPDO Dyess, P.O. Box 545, Dyess AFB, Abilene, TX 79607
ICX,
>P.O. Box 2792, Abilene, TX 79604 (F, V, H)

J.D. Trs. & Stg.,
>249 Cherry, Abilene, TX 79602 (P, C, F)

DPDO Goodfellow, Goodfellow AFB, TX 76901
American Mayflower Mvg. & St.,
>417 E. Ave. D, San Angelo, TX 76901 (P, C)

DPDO Fort Sam Houston, San Antonio, TX 78234
A & W Transfer & Storage,
>4403 Factory Hill Dr., San Antonio, TX 78219 (P, C)

Dealers Transit Inc.,
>602½ N.W.W. White, San Antonio, TX 78219 (F, V, H)

**DPDO San Antonio, Bldg. 3030, East Kelly, Kelly AFB,
San Antonio, TX 78241**
A & W Transfer & Storage,
>4403 Factory Hill Dr., San Antonio, TX 78219 (P, C)

Dealers Transit Inc.,
>602½ N.W.W. White, San Antonio, TX 78219 (F, V, H)

DPDO Laughlin AFB, Del Rio, TX 78840
Allen Transfer & Storage,
>509 Converse, Del Rio, TX 78840 (P, C, V)

Basse Truck Lines,
>203 Avenue O, Del Rio, Tx 78840 (F)

**DPDO Reese, P.O. Box 677, Reese AFB,
Lubbock, TX 79489**
Delta Moving & Storage,
>1333 E. 44, Lubbock, TX 79404 (P, C, F, V, H)

DPDO Sheppard, Sheppard AFB, Wichita Falls, TX 76311
L.J. Trucking Company,
    P.O. Box 581, Burkburnett, TX 76354 (P, C, F, V, H)

Naval Inactive Ship Storage Facility, Orange, TX
    Satellited on DPDO, Ft. Polk LA
Mercury Freight Lines, Inc.,
    P.O. Box 807, Orange, TX 77630 (F)
Burris Transfer & Storage,
    660 Fannin St., P.O. Box 5133, Beaumont, TX 77706 (P,C)

DPDO Texarkana, Red River Army Depot, New Boston, TX 75570
Belter Cartage Service,
    Kansas City, MO (P, C, F, V, H)

DPDO Webb, Webb AFB, TX 79720
McAllister Trucking Co.
    3604 W. Hwy., Big Spring, TX 79720 (F, V, H)
Moorehead Transfer & Storage,
    100 Johnson, Big Spring, TX 79720 (P, C)

UTAH

DPDO Hill, Hill AFB, Ogden, UT 84406
IML Freight Inc.,
    6024 S. College, Ft. Collins, CO 80521 (F)
Union Pacific Railroad,
    2500 Wall Ave., Ogden, UT 84401 (F)

DPDO Tooele, Tooele Army Depot, Tooele, UT 84074
IML Freight Inc.,
    2175 S. 3270 W., Salt Lake City, UT 84119 (F, C, P, I)

VIRGINIA

DPDO Belvoir, Meade Rd., Bldg. S-1976, Fort Belvoir, VA 22060
Estes Express Company,
   Backlick Rd., Springfield, VA (F)
Hilldrup Transfer & Storage Co.,
   Box 1835, Quantico, VA 22134 (P, C)

DPDHA, Camp Allen Salvage Yard, Norfolk, VA 23511
A.J. Beniato,
   5600 E. Va. Beach Blvd., Norfolk, VA (P, C, F)

**DPDO Dahlgren, Naval Surface Weapons Ctr. Dahlgren Lab.,
   Dahlgren, VA 22448**
Service Transfer, Inc.,
   2811 Fall Hill Ave., Fredericksburg, VA (F)

DPDO Quantico, P.O. Box 245, Quantico, VA 22134
Estes Express Lines,
   P.O. Box 667, Springfield, VA 22150 (F)
Hilldrup Transfer & Storage,
   Box 1835, Quantico, VA 22134 (P, C)

Radford Army Ammunition Plant, Radford, VA 24141
Yarbrough Trans. Co. of Va.,
   P.O. Box 853, Roanoke, VA (P, C, F, H)

**DPDO Richmond, Defense General Supply Ctr., Warehouse 3,
   Richmond, VA 23297**
Brooks Transfer & Storage,
   1301 N. Blvd., Richmond, VA 23230 (P, C, F)

WASHINGTON

DPDO Lewis, Fort Lewis, WA 98433
Global Moving & Storage Inc.,
   P.O. Box 99357, Lakewood Industrial Park,
   9612 47th Ave., SW, Tacoma, WA 98499 (F, C, P, I)

WISCONSIN

Badger Army Ammunition Plant, Baraboo, WI 53913
Consolidated Freightways,
   2116 Pennsylvania Ave., Madison, WI (F)

DPDO Sparta, Fort McCoy, Bldg. 2184, Sparta, WI 54656
Gerke Transfer,
   Rt. 3, Toma, WI 54660 (P, C, F)

DEPARTMENT OF DEFENSE
DEFENSE LOGISTICS AGENCY

SALE NO. 31-0007

BID OPENING:

10 OCT - 2:00 P.M.

SEALED BID

Offering...

BOAT

FOR SALE SITE AND MAILING ADDRESS SEE PAGE NO. 9

FOR FURTHER INFORMATION SEE INSIDE

CHAPTER 16

ITEMS SOLD AS SURPLUS
BY THE DEPARTMENT OF DEFENSE

— Agricultural Machinery and Equipment —

Class No.

3710   Soil Preparation Equipment (including planting equipment and cultivating equipment)

3720   Harvesting Equipment

3740   Pest, Disease, and Frost Control Equipment

3750   Gardening Implements and Tools

— Agricultural Supplies —

8710   Forage and Feed

— Aircraft and Airframe Structural Components —

Types of aircraft that are authorized for sale are commercial type, cargo, and passenger carrying in each of the following property categories number 1510A, 1510B, 1510C and 1520. Military type aircraft must be demilitarized and sold for recovery of basic metal content, parts and components (see property category number 9680F).

1510A   Single Engine Aircraft

1510B   Twin Engine Aircraft

1510C   Multi-Engine Aircraft

1520   Aircraft, Rotary Wing (e.g., helicopters)

1550   Drones (e.g., complete drones used as targets, training, surveillance, etc.)

1560A   Airframe Structural Components, etc., peculiar to Single Engine Aircraft

1560B   Airframe Structural Components, etc., peculiar to Multi-Engine Aircraft

1560C   Airframe Structural Components, etc., peculiar to Helicopters

— Aircraft Components and Accessories —

1610   Aircraft Propellers and Component Parts

Class No.

1615   Helicopter Rotor Blades, Drive Mechanisms and Components (e.g., rotors, yokes, blades, blade sets, clutches, transmissions, etc.)

1620   Aircraft Landing Gear Components

1630   Aircraft Wheel and Brake Systems

1650   Aircraft Hydraulic, Vacuum, and Deicing System Components

1660   Aircraft Air Conditioning, Heating, and Pressurizing Equipment

1670   Parachutes and Aerial Pick Up, Delivery, and Cargo Tie Down Equipment

1680   Miscellaneous Aircraft Accessories and Components

— Aircraft Launching, Landing, and Ground Handling Equipment —

1710   Aircraft Arresting, Barrier, and Barricade Equipment (e.g., shipboard and land based types)

1720   Aircraft Launching Equipment (e.g., catapults, etc.)

1730   Aircraft and Space Vehicle Ground Handling and Servicing Equipment (includes energizers, engine preheaters, mooring assemblies, beaching equipment, passenger loading ramps, maintenance platforms, specialized slings, hoists, etc.)

1740   Airfield Specialized Trucks and Trailers

— Alarm and Signal Systems —

6320   Shipboard Alarm and Signal Systems (e.g., motor order indicators, ship's draft indicators, ship's speed indicators, total revolution indicators, etc.)

6340   Aircraft Alarm and Signal System (e.g., aircraft crew warning signals, audible landing gear alarms, oil pressure warning signals, etc.)

6350   Miscellaneous Alarm and Signal Systems (includes alarm bells; buzzers; fire alarm switchboards; foghorns; siren alarms; traffic, transit railroad signal systems and warning devices)

— Bearings —

3110   Bearings, Antifriction, Unmounted

Class No.

3120	Bearings, Plain, Unmounted
3130	Bearings, Mounted

— Books and Other Publications —

7610	Books and Pamphlets

— Brushes, Paints, Sealers, and Adhesives —

8010	Paints, Dopes, Varnishes, and Related Products
8030	Preservative and Sealing Compounds
8040	Adhesives

— Chemicals and Chemical Products —

6810	Chemicals (includes nonmedicinal chemical elements and compounds, such as naphtha solvents, acetone, etc.)
6830	Gases: Compressed and Liquefied (e.g., technical nitrogen, oxygen, fuel gases, etc.)
6840	Pest Control Agents and Disinfectants (includes insect repellents, fungicides, insecticides, rodenticides, weed killers, etc.)
6850	Miscellaneous Chemical Specialties (e.g., antifogging compound, anti-freeze, deicing fluid, etc.)

— Cleaning Equipment and Supplies —

7910	Floor Polishers and Vacuum Cleaners
7930	Cleaning and Polishing Compounds and Preparations

— Clothing and Individual Equipment —

8405	Outerwear, Men's (e.g., breeches, raincoats, field jackets, knit caps, overalls, parkas, ponchos, etc.)
8410	Outerwear, Women's (e.g., blouses, raincoats, dresses, etc.)
8415	Clothing, Special Purpose (includes safety, protective, and athletic clothing, etc.)
8420	Underwear and Nightwear, Men's
8340	Footwear, Men's
8435	Footwear, Women's
8440	Hosiery, Handwear, and Clothing Accessories: Men's
8445	Hosiery, Handwear, and Clothing Accessories: Women's
8460	Luggage
8465	Individual Equipment (e.g., ammunition belts, intrenching tool carriers, sleeping and duffel bags, flying goggles, sun

glasses, etc.)

8475   Specialized Flight Clothing and Accessories

— Communication Equipment —

5805   Telephone and Telegraph Equipment

5815   Teletype and Facsimile Equipment

5820   Radio and Television Communication Equipment, except Airborne (excludes home-type radio and television equipment)

5821   Radio and Television Communication Equipment, Airborne

5825   Radio Navigation Equipment, except Airborne

5826   Radio Navigation Equipment, Airborne

5830   Intercommunication and Public Address System, except Airborne

5831   Intercommunication and Public Address Systems, Airborne

5835   Sound Recording and Reproducing Equipment (excludes phonographs, home-type, and dictation machines)

5840   Radar Equipment, except Airborne

5841   Radar Equipment, Airborne

5845   Underwater Sound Equipment (includes only communication types of infrared equipment)

5895   Miscellaneous Communication Equipment

— Construction and Building Materials —

5610   Mineral Construction Materials, Bulk

5640   Wallboard, Building Paper, and Thermal Insulation Materials

5650   Roofing and Siding Materials

5660   Fencing, Fences, and Gates

5670   Architectural and Related Metal Products (includes door frames, fixed fire escapes, grating, staircases, window sash, etc.)

5680   Miscellaneous Construction Materials (includes metal lath, airplane landing mats, traction mats, tile, brick, nonmetallic pipe and conduit)

Class No.

— Construction, Mining, Excavating, and — Highway Maintenance Equipment

3805   Earth Moving and Excavating Equipment

3810   Cranes and Crane-Shovels (excludes barge-mounted cranes)

3815   Crane and Crane-Shovel Attachments

3820   Mining, Rock Drilling, Earth Boring, and Related Equipment

3825   Road Clearing and Cleaning Equipment

3830   Truck and Tractor Attachments (includes equipment for mounting on trucks and tractors, such as bulldozers, augers, blades, snowplows, sweepers, etc.)

3835   Petroleum Production and Distribution Equipment (includes wellheads, pumping equipment, and gas distribution equipment)

3895   Miscellaneous Construction Equipment (e.g., asphalt heaters and kettles, concrete mixers, pile drivers, cable laying, lashing, spinning, and reeling equipment, etc.)

— Containers, Packaging, and Packing Supplies —

8105   Bags and Sacks

8110   Drums and Cans

8115   Boxes, Cartons and Crates

8120   Gas Cylinders (e.g., compressed gas and acetylene cylinders, liquid gas tanks, etc.)

8125   Bottles and Jars

8130   Reels and Spools

8135   Packaging and Packing Bulk Materials (e.g., baling wire, waterproof barriers, corrugated and wrapping paper, etc.)

8140   Ammunition and Nuclear Ordnance Boxes, Packages, and Special Containers

8145   Shipping and Storage Containers (reusable and repairable containers designed for shipping and storage of equipment)

— Electric Wire, and Power and Distribution Equipment —

6105   Motors, Electrical

6110   Electrical Control Equipment

6115   Generators and Generator Sets, Electrical

Class No.

6120   Transformers: Distribution and Power Station
6125   Converters, Electrical
6130   Power Conversion Equipment, Electrical
6135   Batteries, Primary
6140   Batteries, Secondary
6145   Wire and Cable, Electrical
6150   Miscellaneous Electric Power and Distribution Equipment

— Electrical and Electronic Equipment Components —

5905   Resistors
5910   Capacitors
5915   Filters and Networks
5920   Fuses and Lightning Arresters
5925   Circuit Breakers
5930   Switches
5935   Connectors, Electrical
5940   Lugs, Terminals, and Terminal Strips
5945   Relays, Contactors, and Solenoids
5950   Coils and Transformers
5955   Piezoelectric Crystals (includes processed unmounted crystals, etc.)
5960   Electron Tubes, Transistors, and Rectifying Crystals
5961   Semi-Conductor Devices and Associated Hardware (e.g., diodes, triodes, etc.)
5965   Headsets, Handsets, Microphones, and Speakers
5970   Electrical Insulators and Insulating Materials
5975   Electrical Hardware and Supplies
5977   Electrical Contact Brushes and Electrodes
5985   Antennas, Waveguides, and Related Equipment
5990   Synchros and Resolvers (includes autosyn motors, selsyn generators, synchro receivers, torque amplifiers, etc.)
5995   Cable Cord, and Wire Assemblies: Communication Equipment
5999   Miscellaneous Electrical and Electronic Components (includes light-switches, microware chokes, permanent magnets, etc.)

— Engine Accessories —

2910   Engine Fuel System Components, Non-aircraft (e.g., fuel tanks, lines, filters and pumps, carburetors, etc.)

2915   Engine Fuel System Components, Aircraft (e.g., fuel pumps, filters, controls, valves, etc.; excludes aircraft fuel tanks)

2920   Engine Electrical System Components, Non-aircraft (e.g., generators, spark plugs, coils, distributors, voltage regulators, ignition harness, starters, magnetos)

2925   Engine Electrical System Components, Aircraft

2930   Engine Cooling System Components, Non-aircraft

2935   Engine Cooling System Components, Aircraft

2940   Engine Air and Oil Filters, Strainers, and Cleaners, Non-aircraft

2945   Engine Air and Oil Filters, Strainers, and Cleaners, Aircraft

2950   Turbosuperchargers

2990   Miscellaneous Engine Accessories, Non-aircraft (excludes electrical starters)

2995   Miscellaneous Engine Accessories, Aircraft

— Engines, Turbines, and Components —

2805   Gasoline Reciprocating Engines, except Aircraft; and Components

2810   Gasoline Reciprocating Engines, Aircraft; and Components (e.g., only aircraft prime mover types)

2815   Diesel Engines and Components

2820   Steam Engines, Reciprocating and Components

2825   Steam Turbines and Components

2835   Gas Turbines and Jet Engines, except Aircraft; and Components (e.g., airborne auxiliary and ground gas turbine power units for aircraft engine starting, etc.

2840   Gas Turbines and Jet Engines, Aircraft and Components (e.g., turbo-prop and turbo-jet engines, etc.)

2845   Rocket Engines and Components

2895   Miscellaneous Compressed Air and Wind Engines; Water Turbines and Wheels; and Components

Class No.

— Explosives —

1375   Demolition Materials (includes items such as dynamite, blasting caps, blasting time fuses, impulse cartridges, etc.)

1376   Bulk Explosives (e.g., packaged solid propellants, explosive loaded devices and components, etc.)

— Fire Control Equipment —

1220   Fire Control Computing Sights and Devices

1240   Optical Sighting and Ranging Equipment (e.g., range and height finders, telescopic sights, optical instruments integrated with fire control equipment)

1260   Fire Control Designating and Indicating Equipment

1265   Fire Control Transmitting and Receiving Equipment, except Airborne

1270   Aircraft Gunnery Fire Control Components

1280   Aircraft Bombing Fire Control Components

1285   Fire Control Radar Equipment, except Airborne

1290   Miscellaneous Fire Control Equipment (includes Control Directors and Systems, Stabilizing Mechanisms, and Sonar Equipment)

— Fire Fighting, Rescue, and Safety Equipment —

4210   Fire Fighting Equipment (including Fire Trucks)

4220   Marine Lifesaving and Diving Equipment (excludes lifesaving boats)

4230   Decontaminating and Impregnating Equipment

4240   Safety and Rescue Equipment

— Food Preparation and Serving Equipment —

7310   Food Cooking, Baking, and Warming Equipment

7320   Kitchen Equipment and Appliances

7330   Kitchen Hand Tools and Utensils

7350   Tableware

7360   Sets, Kits, and Outfits: Food Preparation and Serving

— Fuels, Lubricants, Oils, and Waxes —

9110   Fuels, Solid

9130   Liquid Propellants and Fuels, Petroleum Base

9135   Liquid Propellant Fuels and Oxidizers, Chemical Base

9140	Fuel Oils
9150	Oils and Greases: Cutting, Lubricating, and Hydraulic
9160	Miscellaneous Waxes, Oils and Fats

— Furnace, Steam Plant, and Drying Equipment —

4410	Industrial Boilers
4420	Heat Exchangers and Steam Condensers
4430	Industrial Furnaces, Kilns, Lehrs, and Ovens (excludes food industry ovens, metal heating treating and laboratory type furnaces)
4440	Driers, Dehydrators, and Anhydrators
4450	Industrial Fan and Blower Equipment
4460	Air Purification Equipment (includes electronic precipitators and dust collectors)

— Furniture —

7105	Household Furniture
7110	Office Furniture
7125	Cabinets, Lockers, Bins, and Shelving
7195	Miscellaneous Furniture and Fixtures (e.g., library furniture, cashiers' stands, theatre furniture, etc.)

— Guided Missile Equipment —

1440	Launchers, Guided Missile (e.g., airborne and non-airborne guided missile launchers)
1450	Guided Missile Handling and Servicing Equipment (e.g., specially designed trucks and trailers, slings, hoists, jacks, etc.)

— Hand Tools —

5110	Hand Tools, Edged, Nonpowered
5120	Hand Tools, Nonedged, Nonpowered
5130	Hand Tools, Power Driven
5133	Drill Bits, Counterbores, and Countersinks: Hand and Machine
5136	Taps, Dies, and Collets: Hand and Machine (excludes punching, stamping, and marking dies)
5140	Tool and Hardware Boxes
5180	Sets, Kits, and Outfits of Hand Tools

Class No.

—Hardware and Abrasives —

5305	Screws
5306	Bolts
5307	Studs
5310	Nuts and Washers
5315	Nails, Keys, and Pins
5320	Rivets
5325	Fastening Devices
5330	Packing and Gasket Materials
5340	Miscellaneous Hardware and Metal Screening
5345	Disks and Stones, Abrasive
5350	Abrasive Materials
5355	Knobs and Pointers

— Household and Commercial Furnishings and Appliances —

7210   Household Furnishings (e.g., bed blankets, mattresses, and pillows, etc.)

7240   Household and Commercial Utility Containers

7290   Miscellaneous Household and Commercial Furnishings and Appliances (includes carpets, mats, tile, draperies, awnings, shades, etc.)

— Instruments and Laboratory Equipment —

6605   Navigational Instruments (e.g., Azimuths, gyro compasses, drift meters, navigational computers, aircraft octants, plotting boards, aircraft sextants, marine sextants, etc.)

6610   Flight Instruments (e.g., airspeed indicators, bank and turn indicators, venturi tubes, etc.)

6615   Automatic Pilot Mechanisms and Airborne Gyro Components

6620   Engine Instruments (includes all engine instruments, including aircraft, marine, and vehicular; fuel pressure gages, manifold pressure gages, oil pressure gages, fuel mixture indicators, engine oil and fuel warning devices)

6625   Electrical and Electronic Properties Measuring and Testing Instruments (includes all basic types of test instruments designed for communication and electronic equipment,

Class No.

such as ammeters, voltmeters, ohmmeters, multimeters, and similar instruments, etc.)

6630   Chemical Analysis Instruments (e.g., gas analyzers, hydrometers, etc.)

6635   Physical Properties Testing Equipment (e.g., balancing machines, hardness testers, industrial X-ray machines, magnaflux testing equipment, torque bearing testers, etc.)

6636   Environmental Chambers and Related Equipment (e.g., chambers, wind tunnels, weatherometers, fadeometers, etc.

6640   Laboratory Equipment and Supplies

6645   Time Measuring Instruments

6650   Optical Instruments (e.g., binoculars, microscopes, telescopes, etc.)

6655   Geophysical and Astronomical Instruments (e.g., geodetic, oceanographic, and seismographic instruments, etc.)

6660   Meteorological Instruments and Apparatus (e.g., wind direction and speed detectors, radiosonde sets, meteorological balloons, etc.)

6665   Hazard-Detecting Instruments and Apparatus (e.g., mine detectors, gas detecting equipment, radiac equipment, water testing sets, etc.)

6670   Scales and Balances (e.g., household, industrial, postal, and laboratory scales and balances, etc.)

6675   Drafting, Surveying, and Mapping Instruments

6680   Liquid and Gas Flow, Liquid Level, and Mechanical Motion Measuring Instruments (e.g., electrical counters, engine tachometers, gas and liquid flowmeters, speedometers, etc.)

6685   Pressure, Temperature, and Humidity Measuring and Controlling Instruments (e.g., altimeters, barometers, gages, etc.)

6695   Combination and Miscellaneous Instruments (e.g., recording lie detectors, light-time recorders, meter registers, etc.)

Class No.

— Lighting Fixtures and Lamps —

6210 Indoor and Outdoor Electric Lighting Fixtures
6220 Electric Vehicular Lights and Fixtures (includes automotive, marine, railroad and aircraft fixtures)
6230 Electric Portable and Hand Lighting Equipment
6240 Electric Lamps
6250 Ballasts, Lampholders, and Starters

— Live Animals —

8820 Live Animals (e.g., horses, mules, and working dogs)

— Lumber, Millwork, Plywood, and Veneer —

5510 Lumber and Related Basic Wood Materials (includes plywood, veneer, and millwork)

— Maintenance and Repair Shop Equipment —

4910 Motor Vehicle Maintenance and Repair Shop Specialized Equipment (excludes hand tools)
4920 Aircraft Maintenance and Repair Shop Specialized Equipment
4925 Ammunition Maintenance and Repair Shop Specialized Equipment
4930 Lubrication and Fuel Dispensing Equipment
4931 Fire Control Maintenance and Repair Shop Specialized Equipment
4933 Weapons Maintenance and Repair Shop Specialized Equipment
4935 Guided Missile Maintenance, Repair, and Checkout Specialized Equipment (includes checkout equipment and test equipment specially designed for use with guided missiles and guided remote control systems)
4940 Miscellaneous Maintenance and Repair Shop Specialized Equipment (includes paint spraying equipment)
4960 Space Vehicle Maintenance, Repair, and Checkout Specialized Equipment (includes checkout and test equipment specially designed for use with space vehicles, including remote control systems)

Class No.

— Materials Handling Equipment —

3910   Conveyers

3920   Material Handling Equipment, Nonself-Propelled (includes dolly trucks, pushcarts, handcarts, wheelbarrows, hand trucks, and material handling trailers)

3930   Warehouse Trucks and Tractors, Self-Propelled (includes fork lift trucks, straddle trucks, cab, body, and frame structural components and springs, etc.)

3940   Blocks, Tackle, Rigging, and Slings

3950   Winches, Hoists, Cranes, and Derricks

3960   Elevators and Escalators

3990   Miscellaneous Materials Handling Equipment (includes skids and pallets)

— Measuring Tools —

5210   Measuring Tools, Craftsmen's

5220   Inspection Gages and Precision Layout Tools

5280   Sets, Kits, and Outfits of Measuring Tools

— Mechanical Power Transmission Equipment —

3010   Torque Converters and Speed Changers

3020   Gears, Pulleys, Sprockets, and Transmission Chain

3030   Belting, Drive Belts, Fan Belts, and Accessories

3040   Miscellaneous Power Transmission Equipment

— Medical, Dental, and Veterinary Equipment and Supplies —

6505   Drugs, Biologicals, and Official Reagents

6510   Surgical Dressing Materials

6515   Medical and Surgical Instruments, Equipment, and Supplies

6520   Dental Instruments, Equipment, and Supplies

6525   X-Ray Equipment and Supplies: Medical, Dental, Veterinary

6530   Hospital Furniture, Equipment, Utensils, and Supplies

6540   Opticians' Instruments, Equipment, and Supplies

6545   Medical Sets, Kits, and Outfits

— Metal Bars, Sheets, and Shapes —

9505   Wire, Nonelectrical, Iron and Steel

9510   Bars and Rods, Iron and Steel

Class No.

9515   Plate, Sheet, and Strip: Iron and Steel
9520   Structural Shapes, Iron and Steel
9525   Wire, Nonelectrical, Nonferrous Base Metal
9530   Bars and Rods, Nonferrous Base Metal
9535   Plate, Sheet, Strip, and Foil: Nonferrous Base Metal
9540   Structural Shapes, Nonferrous Base Metal
9545   Plate, Sheet, Strip, Foil, and Wire: Precious Metal

— Metalworking Machinery —

3411   Boring Machines
3412   Broaching Machines
3413   Drilling Machines
3414   Gear Cutting and Finishing Machines
3415   Grinding Machines
3416   Lathes (excludes speed lathes)
3417   Milling Machines
3418   Planers
3419   Miscellaneous Machine Tools (e.g., shapers, speed lathes, etc.)
3422   Rolling Mills and Drawing Machines
3424   Metal Heat Treating and Non-Thermal Treating Equipment
3426   Metal Finishing Equipment
3431   Electric Arc Welding Equipment (excludes welding supplies and associated equipment)
3432   Electric Resistance Welding Equipment
3433   Gas Welding, Heat Cutting, and Metalizing Equipment
3436   Welding Positioners and Manipulators
3438   Miscellaneous Welding Equipment
3439   Miscellaneous Welding, Soldering, and Brazing Supplies and Accessories
3441   Bending and Forming Machines
3442   Hydraulic and Pneumatic Presses, Power Driven
3443   Mechanical Presses, Power Driven (includes forging presses)
3444   Manual Presses
3445   Punching and Shearing Machines
3446   Forging Machinery and Hammers (excludes forging presses)

Class No.

3447	Wire and Metal Ribbon Forming Machines
3448	Riveting Machines (excludes power driven hand riveting machines)
3449	Miscellaneous Secondary Metal Forming and Cutting Machines
3450	Machine Tools, Portable
3455	Cutting Tools for Machine Tools (excludes flame cutting tools)
3456	Cutting and Forming Tools for Secondary Metalworking Machinery
3460	Machine Tool Accessories
3465	Production Jigs, Fixtures, and Templates
3470	Machine Shop Sets, Kits, and Outfits

— Motor Vehicles, Trailers, and Cycles —

2310A	Passenger Motor Vehicles (e.g., sedans, station wagons, etc.)
2310B	Ambulances and Hearses
2310C	Buses
2320A	Trucks and Truck Tractors one ton and heavier capacity
2320B	Amphibian Vehicles
2320C	Jeeps and all four-wheel drive vehicles of less than one ton capacity
2320D	Trucks (pickups, step-vans, panel, delivery, etc.) with two-wheel drive of less than one ton capacity
2330	Trailers (e.g., semitrailers, house trailers, semitrailer dollies, etc.)
2340	Motorcycles, Motor Scooters, and Bicycles

— Musical Instruments, Phonographs, and Home-Type Radios —

7710	Musical Instruments (includes musical instrument parts and accessories)
7730	Phonographs, Radios, and Television Sets: Home-Type

— Nonmetallic Fabricated Materials —

9310	Paper and Paperboard
9320	Rubber Fabricated Materials
9330	Plastics Fabricated Materials
9340	Glass Fabricated Materials

Class No.

9350   Refractories and Fire Surfacing Materials

9390   Miscellaneous Fabricated Nonmetallic Materials (e.g., asbestos fabricated materials, cork and fibre sheets, etc.)

— Nuclear Ordnance Equipment —

1190   Specialized Test and Handling Equipment, Nuclear Ordnance (e.g., specially designed trucks and trailers, slings and hoists, etc.)

— Office Machines and Data Processing Equipment —

7410   Punched Card System Machines (e.g., key punch, sorting and tabulating machines, etc.)

7420   Accounting and Calculating Machines

7430   Typewriters and Office Type Composing Machines

7440   Automatic Data Processing Systems: Industrial, Scientific, and Office Types (e.g., electronic data counters, digital computers, magnetic tape, etc.)

7450   Office Type Sound Recording and Reproducing Machines (e.g., dictating machines, sound recorders, sound recording tape, transcribing machines, etc.)

7460   Visible Record Equipment (e.g., visible index cabinet files and rotary files, etc.)

7490   Miscellaneous Office Machines (e.g., cash registers, check signing and writing machines, label printing machines, etc.)

— Office Supplies and Devices —

7510   Office Supplies

7520   Office Devices and Accessories

7530   Stationery and Record Forms (excludes standard forms approved for Government wide use)

— Photographic Equipment —

6710   Cameras, Motion Picture

6720   Cameras, Still Picture

6730   Photographic Projection Equipment

6740   Photographic Developing and Finishing Equipment

6750   Photographic Supplies

6760   Photographic Equipment and Accessories

6770   Film, Processed

6780   Photographic Sets, Kits, and Outfits

— Pipe, Tubing, Hose, and Fittings —

4710   Pipe and Tube (includes metal pipe and tube, rigid pipe and tube of plastic, synthetic rubber, or other non-metallic material for other than underground, electrical, or laboratory use)

4720   Hose and Tubing, Flexible (includes metallic and non-metallic flexible hose and tubing, hydraulic, air, chemical, fuel and oil hose assemblies)

4730   Fittings, and Specialties: Hose, Pipe, and Tube (includes plumbing fittings and specialties, lubrication fittings, pipe joints, including expansion joints, etc.)

— Plumbing, Heating, and Sanitation Equipment —

4510   Plumbing Fixtures and Accessories

4520   Space Heating Equipment and Domestic Water Heaters

4530   Fuel Burning Equipment Units

4540   Miscellaneous Plumbing, Heating, and Sanitation Equipment (includes incinerators, destructors, septic tanks, and garbage disposal units)

— Prefabricated Structures and Scaffolding —

5410   Prefabricated and Portable Buildings

5420   Bridges, Fixed and Floating (excludes pontoons and floating docks)

5430   Storage Tanks

5440   Scaffolding Equipment and Concrete Forms

5445   Prefabricated Tower Structures

5450   Miscellaneous Prefabricated Structures (includes bleachers, grandstands, etc.)

— Primary Metal Products —

9630   Additive Metal Materials and Master Alloys (e.g., additives aluminum, copper, nickel alloying ferroboron, ferronickel, ferrovanadium, etc.)

9640   Iron and Steel Primary and Semi-finished Products (e.g., ingots, pigs, billets, blooms, muck bar, skelp, etc.)

Class No.

9650 Nonferrous Base Metal Refinery and Intermediate Forms (e.g., ingots, slabs, mercury, etc.)

— Pumps and Compressors —

4310 Compressors and Vacuum Pumps

4320 Power and Hand Pumps

4330 Centrifugals Separators, and Pressure and Vacuum Filters

— Railway Equipment —

2210 Locomotives

2220 Rail Cars (e.g., trailed cars, self-propelled cars, etc.)

2230 Right-of-Way Construction and Maintenance Equipment, Railroad (e.g., locomotive cranes, snowplows, tamping machines, etc.)

2240 Locomotive and Rail Car Accessories and Components

2250 Track Materials, Railroad (e.g., rails, frogs, fish plates, etc.)

— Recreational and Athletic Equipment —

7810 Athletic and Sporting Equipment (e.g., basketballs, footballs, boxing gloves, etc.)

7830 Recreational and Gymnastic Equipment

— Refrigeration and Air Conditioning Equipment —

4110 Self-Contained Refrigeration Units and Accessories

4120 Self-Contained Air Conditioning Units and Accessories

4130 Refrigeration and Air Conditioning Plants and Components

4140 Fans and Air Circulators, Nonindustrial

— Rope, Cable, Chain, and Fittings —

4010 Chain and Wire Rope

4020 Fiber Rope, Cordage, and Twine

4030 Fittings for Rope, Cable, and Chain

—Scrap and Waste —

8305A Textiles including Synthetic Fabric (e.g., canvas, parachutes, etc.)

9450A Paper (e.g., newsprint, manila cards, etc.)

9450B Rubber (e.g., tires and tubes all types, etc.)

9450C Miscellaneous (e.g., leather, plastic, fiberglass, etc.)

9450D Exposed Film and Spent Hypo Solution

Class No.

9450E   Waste Oil, Jet Fuels, Paints, Chemicals, Waxes, and Lubricants

9450F   Food Waste (e.g., garbage, grease, fat, bones, contaminated foods, etc.)

9450G   Industrial Diamond Containing Materials (e.g., honing sticks, grinding wheels, swarf, sludge, etc.)

9660A   Precious Metals, All Types (e.g., silver, amalgam, platinum, palladium, rhodium, etc., but excludes hypo solutions)

9660B   Gold and Silver Plated or Brazed on Base Metal (includes gold and silver flashed material, but excludes gold, silver, gold alloys, silver alloys, gold and silver filled materials which are classified under Class 9660A)

9670C   Cast Iron (includes breakable, burnt, borings)

9670D   Prepared Heavy Melting Steel

9670E   Unprepared Heavy Melting Steel

9670F   Prepared Light Steel (black and/or galvanized)

9670G   Unprepared Light Steel (black and/or galvanized)

9670H   Unprepared Mixed Heavy and Light Steel

9670J   Turnings and Borings (steel and/or wrought iron)

9670K   Stainless Steel Alloys, Magnetic and Nonmagnetic (e.g., 300 and 400 series types except types 310 and 446 of the American Iron and Steel Institute)

9670L   High Temperature Alloys: Nickel and Cobalt Base which are Copper Free (e.g., inconel, hastelloy, nimonic, multimet, waspalloy, stellite, etc., including molybdenum alloys, tungsten alloys, titanium alloys, high speed tool steel, and types 310 and 446 of the American Iron and Steel Institute)

9680B   Copper, Copper-Base Alloys and Copper Containing Materials (e.g., brass, bronze, monel, cupro-nickel, nickel-silver, copper wire (bare, insulated and lead covered), shell cases, babbitt-lined brass bearings, etc., but excludes copper-bearing materials)

9680C   Copper-Bearing Materials (e.g., motors, armatures, generators, etc., but excludes electrical and electronic materials)

Class No.

9680D   Miscellaneous Electrical and Electronic Materials (includes steel or aluminum armored cable, etc., but excludes copper- bearing materials)

9680E   Aluminum and Aluminum Alloys (excludes material in Class 9680F)

9680F   Aircraft sold for recovery of basic metal content, parts and components (includes aircraft for scrapping and/or sweating)

9680G   Magnesium Alloys

9680H   Lead, Lead-Base Alloys, Antimony, Zinc and Zinc Alloys (includes vehicle, aircraft and submarine lead-acid type storage batteries)

9680J   Bullet and Projectile Metals (to be recovered from target, artillery and bombing ranges)

9680K   Storage Batteries (nickel-iron-alkaline types)

9680L   Storage Batteries (silver-zinc, nickel-cadmium and mercury types)

9680M   Tin and Alloys (includes tin-base babbitt metal and block tin pipe, but excludes tin cans and terneplate)

— Service and Trade Equipment —

3510   Laundry and Dry Cleaning Equipment

3520   Shoe Repairing Equipment

3530   Industrial Sewing Machines and Mobile Textile Repair Shops (excludes shoe sewing machines)

3540   Wrapping and Packaging Machinery

3550   Vending and Coin Operated Machines

3590   Miscellaneous Service and Trade Equipment (includes barber chairs, kits, hair clippers and shears, etc.)

— Ship and Marine Equipment —

2010   Ship and Boat Propulsion Components (excludes engines and turbines)

2020   Rigging and Rigging Gear

2030   Deck Machinery

2040   Marine Hardware and Hull Items (e.g., anchors, hatches, rudders, oars, etc.)

Class No.

2050   Buoys

2090   Miscellaneous Ship, Marine, and Commercial Fishing Equipment (includes sails, marine furniture, ladders, etc.)

— Ships, Small Craft, Pontoons, and Floating Docks —

1905A   Aircraft Carriers (for scrapping only)

1905B   Battleships, Cruisers, Destroyers (for scrapping only)

1905C   Landing Ships (e.g., LST, LSM, LSMR, LSSL, etc.)

1905D   Minehunters, Minesweepers, Minelayers

1905E   Submarines (for scrapping only)

1905F   Landing Craft (e.g., LCVP, LCPL, LCM, etc.)

1910   Transport Vessels, Passenger and Troop

1915   Cargo and Tanker Vessels

1925A   Ferry

1925B   Harbor Utility Craft

1925C   Repair Ships

1925D   Tugs (e.g., YTB, YTL, ATA, etc.)

1930A   Fuel Barge, Gasoline Barge, Water Barge

1930B   Lighters (open and covered)

1935   Barges and Lighters, Special Purpose (e.g., derrick, pipe-driver, torpedo testing barges, barge-mounted cranes, etc.)

1940B   Patrol Craft (e.g., PC, PCS, SC, YP, PCE, etc.)

1940C   Seaplane Tenders

1940D   Small Craft under 40 feet in length powered and non-powered (e.g., lifeboats, rowboats, whaleboats, motor launches, etc.)

1945   Pontoons and Floating Docks (e.g., pontoon ramps, etc.)

1950   Floating Dry Docks

1990   Miscellaneous (all other vessels and service craft not included in property category numbers 1905A through 1950

— Special Industry Machinery —

3605   Food Products Machinery and Equipment (excludes kitchen and galley equipment)

3610   Printing, Duplicating, and Bookbinding Equipment

3615   Pulp and Paper Industries Machinery

3620   Rubber Working Machinery

Class No.

3625	Textile Industries Machinery
3635	Crystal and Glass Industries Machinery
3645	Leather Tanning and Leather Working Industries Machinery
3650	Chemical and Pharmaceutical Products Manufacturing Machinery
3655	Gas Generating Equipment (excludes meteorological equipment)
3680	Foundry Machinery, Related Equipment and Supplies (e.g., molding machines, tumbling mills, foundry dextrine, core paste, etc.)
3685	Specialized Metal Container Manufacturing Machinery and Related Equipment
3690	Specialized Ammunition and Ordnance Machinery and Related Equipment (e.g., ammunition and explosives loading machinery, small arms ammunition, artillery and antiaircraft shell manufacturing machinery, etc.)
3695	Miscellaneous Special Industry Machinery (includes specialized logging equipment, petroleum refinery machinery, shoemaking machinery, optical goods manufacturing machinery, clay and concrete products industries machinery, etc.)

— Textiles —

8305B	Textile Fabrics (e.g., airplane cloth, burlap, canvas, cotton cloth, elastic webbing, etc.)
8340	Tents and Tarpaulins

— Tires and Tubes —

2610	Tires and Tubes, Pneumatic, except Aircraft
2620	Tires and Tubes, Pneumatic, Aircraft
2630	Tires, Solid and Cushion (includes rubber track laying treads)
2640	Tire Rebuilding and Tire and Tube Repair Materials (excludes vulcanizing machinery and equipment)

— Tractors —

2410	Tractors, Full Track, Low Speed (e.g., caterpillar and crawler, etc.)

Class No.

2420	Tractors, Wheeled (e.g., agricultural and industrial wheeled tractors, etc.)
2430	Tractors, Track Laying, High Speed

— Training Aids and Devices —

6910	Training Aids (e.g., cutaway models, map reading instruction kits, scale models, vehicle training aids, etc.)
6920	Armament Training Devices (e.g., target panels, rifle targets, silhouette targets, etc.)
6930	Operational Training Devices (e.g., link trainers, flight simulators, etc.)
6940	Communication Training Devices (e.g., telephone training aids, electronic circuit trainers, etc.)

— Valves —

4810	Valves, Powered
4820	Valves, Nonpowered

— Vehicular Equipment Components —

2510	Vehicular Cab, Body, and Frame Structural Components (e.g., automobile, truck and trailer bodies, frames, etc.)
2520	Vehicular Power Transmission Components (e.g., transmissions, clutches, drive shafts, differentials, power take-offs, hydraulic motors, universal joints, etc.)
2530	Vehicular Brake, Steering, Axle, Wheel, and Track Components (e.g., wheel and brake assemblies, track assemblies, steering assemblies, etc.)
2540	Vehicular Furniture and Accessories (e.g., heaters, de-frosters, winterization kits, seat assemblies, mirrors, curtains, etc.)
2590	Miscellaneous Vehicular Components (e.g., a-frames, bulldozer blades, crane booms, etc.)

— Water Purification and Sewage Treatment Equipment —

4610	Water Purification Equipment (includes filtration equipment and lifesaving water stills)
4620	Water Distillation Equipment, Marine and Industrial
4630	Sewage Treatment Equipment

Class No.

— Weapons (Accessories) —

1005   Holsters, slings, small arms accessories (all firearms and all repair parts thereto, bayonets, bayonet-knives are not available for sale)

— Woodworking Machinery and Equipment —

3210   Sawmill and Planing Mill Machinery

3220   Woodworking Machines (excludes hand held power driven tools)

3230   Tools and Attachments for Woodworking Machinery

INDEX

Airports. 48

Auctions
   Department of Defense. 28
   G.S.A.. 19
   Canadian Government 62
   Customs Service 57
   Postal 59

Belgium
   Local Information. 13

Bidders Services 31

Bids
   Bid Deposit 27
   Bid Deposit Bond 27
   Sealed Bid 27
   Spot Bid 28

Canadian Government Surplus
   Main Office 61
   Public Auctions. 62
   Qualifications of Bidders. 62
   Retail Sales 62
   Sealed Bids. 62

Construction Equipment. 21

Consumer Items 11

Contractor Inventory
   Department of Navy 22
   Regions. 21

Customs Service
   Auctions 57

Department of Defense
   Qualifications of Bidders. 13
   Surplus Sales Central Office. . . .11
   Surplus Sales Regional Offices . .12

Domestic Sales
   Department of Defense. 11
   G.S.A.. 19

Donation Program
   Qualifications. 47
   State Agencies 49

Educational Activities 48

Electronic Equipment
   Identification 37

European Region
   Department of Defense. 13

France
   Local Information. 14

General Services Administration
   Qualifications of Bidders. 20
   Regional Sales Offices 19

Germany
   Local Information. 14

Greece
   Local Information. 14

Guam
   Local Information. 15

Hawaii
   Local Information. 15

Health Activities 48

Holland
   Local Information. 14

Importing Instructions 17

Invitation for Bids (I.F.B.) 27

Italy
   Local Information. 15

Japan

    Local Information 15

Joint Electronics Type

    Designation System 37

Korea

    Local Information 15

Navy Department 22

Okinawa

    Local Information 15

Pacific Region 15

Packing

    Bidders Service 31

    Packing Companies 63

Payments 27

Philippines

    Local Information 15

Postal Service

    Auctions 59

Public Agencies 47

Publications

    Packers and Shippers 63

    Technical Manuals 33

Sale Methods

    Negotiated Sales 29

    Retail Sales 29

Shipping

    Bidders Service 31

    Shipping Companies 63

Spain

    Local Information 14

Technical Manuals 33

Thailand

    Local Information 15

United Kingdom

    Local Information 14

BIBLIOGRAPHY

Portions of this book are copied from or make reference to the following:

1. "Buying Government Surplus Personal Property":
   General Services Administration,
   Federal Supply Service, Washington, D.C.

2. "Classes Of Surplus Personal Property Sold By
   The Department Of Defense":
   Defense Supply Agency,
   Defense Property Disposal Service Federal Center,
   Battle Creek, Michigan

3. "Federal Surplus Personal Property Donation Programs":
   General Services Administration,
   Federal Supply Service, Washington, D.C.

4. "How To Buy Surplus Personal Property From
   The Department Of Defense":
   Defense Property Disposal Service,
   Federal Center, Battle Creek, Michigan

5. "Index Of Administrative Publications":
   Headquarters, Department Of The Army,
   Washington, D.C.

6. "Index Of Doctrinal, Training And Organizational Publications":
   Headquarters, Department Of The Army,
   Washington, D.C.

7. "Index Of Supply Catalogs And Supply Manuals":
   Headquarters, Department Of The Army,
   Washington, D.C.

8. **"Index Of Technical Publications":**
Headquarters, Department Of The Army,
Washington, D.C.

9. **"Military Standard Joint Electronics Type Designation System,"**
MIL - STD - 196C:
Department Of Defense, Washington, D.C.

10. **"Sale By Reference":**
Defense Logistics Agency,
Defense Property Disposal Service,
Battle Creek, Michigan

11. **"Terms And Conditions For Buying Government Surplus**
Personal Property":
General Services Administration,
Federal Supply Service, Washington, D.C.

* IMPORTANT *

If you attend a retail sale or an auction you will know what the price of the surplus items are immediately.

However, if the sale is a sealed bid type, you will probably ask yourself the following questions:

How can I know if my bid is far too high or far too low?

Is there any way to find out what similar items have sold for in the past?

To assist the buyers of this book, the Rainbow Publishing Co. has developed a service to help answer these questions.

For free information write to: Rainbow Publishing Co.
P.O. Box 397
Chesterland, Ohio 44026

Rainbow Publishing Co.
P.O. Box 397
Chesterland, Ohio 44026

If you attend a retail sale or an auction you will know what the price of the surplus items are immediately.

However, if the sale is a sealed bid type, you will probably ask yourself the following questions:

    How can I know if my bid is far too high
       or far too low?

    Is there any way to find out what similar
       items have sold for in the past?

To assist the buyers of this book, the Rainbow Publishing Co. has developed a service to help answer these questions.

Mail the attached postcard for further information.

Send me <u>free</u> information about your service.

I want to know what U.S. Government Surplus items have sold for in the past, so that my sealed bids will have an excellent change of being successful.

NAME _____

ADDRESS _____

CITY & STATE _____

ZIP _____
                          Please Print